# THE WRITINGS OF E. M. FORSTER

# THE WRITINGS OF
# E. M. FORSTER

## ROSE MACAULAY

1970

THE HOGARTH PRESS

LONDON

Published by
The Hogarth Press Ltd
42 William IV Street
London WC2

\*

Clarke, Irwin & Co. Ltd
Toronto

*First Published 1938*
*Second Impression 1970*

SBN 7012 0332 3

© Constance Babington Smith 1938

Printed in Great Britain by
William Lewis (Printers) Ltd,
Cardiff

# CONTENTS

# CHAPTER I

WRITERS, like other people, are rooted in
time and place, embedded in, growing and
flowering out of, these conditioning soils, so that
you will only with some pains sort their elements,
disentangle the individual from the background,
and never (I think) quite; indeed, how could you,
since all the background, the march of all the
centuries, the crowding shades of all the dead up
to that moment, of all the living *in* that moment,
charge the lightest spoken word at any given hour,
with their unescapable rhythms, echoes, syn-
theses and purposes? You cannot move writers,
nor artists, nor musicians, nor philosophers, nor
indeed anyone else, about the world or about time,
or even about society, and retain their peculiar
colour: put, for instance, the Restoration play-
wrights into the Middle Ages, Dante into
eighteenth-century England, make Jane Austen
an Elizabethan, Pope a Lake poet, Coleridge an
Augustan, Horace an Athenian of the Periclean
age, Dickens and Thackeray French twentieth-
century novelists. You cannot, because you cannot imagine what in the world they would be like;

7

perhaps in the mode in which they actually functioned they would not function at all; they would
come up as something else; the sap would run differently. Each pushed and shot out his own
branches, conditioned by, growing out of, but
growing beyond, his nursing soil and air. Explore
and analyse as you will, you cannot disentangle the
independent native qualities of writers from the
thousand calling airy voices of their age.

These are platitudes; and all they mean here is
that the writer E. M. Forster, who would have
found some characteristic expression for himself in
any age or land, any economic and social station,
did actually evolve his self-expression in the early
twentieth century as a young Englishman of the
professional classes, whose forbears had for some
generations lived cultured, humane, philanthropic,
comfortable, liberal, nineteenth-century kind of
lives, of the sort lived by the ancestors of so many
of us, and by so few, if any, of ourselves. Gentle,
intelligent, high-minded, high-browed, these ancestors of ours look down on us from drawings and
paintings on our walls, faintly coloured in their
gold frames, their minds set on freeing West
Indian slaves, on lightening child labour, on attending Evangelical conferences, on reading good
books; whatsoever things are pure, lovely, of good
intent, they think, we may be sure, on these things.
In and out of the letters of the females, written in
delicate pointed hands across reams and reams of

paper, stroll our deceased relations, philan-
thropists, bishops, clergy, members of parliament,
Miss Hannah More. It is all serene, humane and
good, and a bad preparation for the savagery and
storms of this age; that is to say, it *looks* serene,
humane and good, for we know that really our
ancestors led lives of the greatest inner turbulence,
the fiercest spiritual and intellectual conflict, the
wildest mental adventure and chaos. But—is it
the cravats, the gentle sweep of the wavy hair, the
faint colouring and soft lines of the portraits ?—
they look down on us for ever tranquil and cool
and well bred, virginal in their gold frames like the
Blessed Damozel at the gold bar, for all they were
not virginal at all, but did richly and unceasingly
bring forth.

E. M. Forster, then, a product of this kind of
liberal bourgeois culture, is also a product of an
upper-middle-class school and university, and conditioned more precisely by the fact that his college
was King's College, Cambridge, and his Triposes
classical and historical. It is apparent that he fell
in love with Cambridge. His second novel, *The
Longest Journey*, is partly a glorification of university undergraduate life, as being nearer the
true and shining world of reality than is the dark,
chaotic muddle and falsity of most life outside.
Or, anyhow, as holding the password to that
world. A year or two after leaving Cambridge,
Rickie Elliot, in *The Longest Journey*, is engaged to

a mean, commonplace, worldly and stupid young woman who drags him intellectually, morally and spiritually down, making him do the mean and stupid things that she desires. He is returning on an omnibus from seeing a kindly editor who has rejected a story of his.

> " As he rumbled westward, his face was drawn, and his eyes moved quickly to the right and left, as if he would discover something in the squalid fashionable streets—some bird on the wing, some radiant archway, the face of some god beneath a beaver hat. He loved, he was loved, he had seen death and other things ; but the heart of all things was hidden. There was a password and he could not learn it, nor could the kind editor of the *Holborn* teach him. He sighed, and then sighed more piteously. For had he not known the password once—known it and forgotten it already ? "

And, later (Rickie speaking),

> " That's why I pity people who don't go up to Cambridge : not because a University is smart, but because those are the magic years, and—with luck—you see up there what you couldn't see before and mayn't ever see again."

The thing you may see—with luck—up there is Reality: and it is this vision of Reality, this passionate antithesis between the real and the unreal, the true and the false, being and not-being, that gives the whole body of E. M. Forster's work, in whatever *genre*, its unity. The importance he attaches to this antithesis has the urgency of a religion. There is a Way, a Truth, a Life: you may call it, he seems to tell us, Cambridge; or you may, if you look at other expressions of it, call it Wiltshire, or Italy, or various other names; whatever you call it, it is truth and life, and therefore the way, as opposed to humbug, lifeless conventionalism, and dreary muddle. It is, in brief, reality. The crude, hard-drinking young countryman of *The Longest Journey*, Stephen Wonham, the grave young man George Emerson of *A Room with a View*, the young Italian bounder Gino of *Where Angels Fear to Tread*, the gay nymph Miss Beaumont of *Other Kingdom*, who, fleeing from her pompous lover, turns into a beech tree, the quiet, clear-seeing elderly ladies, Mrs. Wilcox and Mrs. Moore of *Howards End* and *A Passage to India*, though none of them has been to Cambridge, yet stand on the Cambridge side of the gulf that divides Cambridge from Sawston, reality from sham, life from non-existence.

" She was not there. She has no existence," says Stewart Ansell, the scornful philosopher of *The Longest Journey*, of Agnes Pembroke, the handsome young woman with whom his unfortunate friend has fallen in love. Agnes is not there; she is not " saved." Cambridge is one of Mr. Forster's symbols for the saved state.

" The earth," says Ansell, " is full of tiny societies, and Cambridge is one of them. All the societies are narrow, but some are good and some are bad—just as one house is beautiful inside and another ugly. . . . The good societies say, ' I tell you to do this because I am Cambridge.' The bad ones say, ' I tell you to do this because I am the great world '—not because I am Peckham, or Billingsgate, or Park Lane, but ' because I am the great world.' They lie."

Many years later Mr. Forster writes of Cambridge again, as it affected Goldsworthy Lowes Dickinson.

" As Cambridge filled up with friends, it acquired a magic quality. Body and spirit, reason and emotion, work and play, architecture and scenery, laughter and seriousness, life and art —these pairs which are elsewhere contrasts were there fused into one. People and books reinforced one another, intelligence joined hands with affection, speculation became a passion, and discussion was made profound by love. When Goldie speaks of this magic fusion, he illumines more lives than his own, and he seems not only to epitomize Cambridge but to amplify it, and to make it the heritage of many who will never go there in the flesh."

And again, of a Cambridge discussion society:

" The young men seek truth rather than victory, they are willing to abjure an opinion when it is proved untenable, they do not try to score off one another, they do not feel diffidence too high a price to pay for integrity ; and according to some observers that is why Cambridge has played, comparatively speaking, so small a part in the control of world affairs. Certainly these societies represent the very antithesis of the rotarian spirit. No one who has once felt their power will ever become a good mixer or a yes-man. Their influence, when it goes wrong, leads to self-consciousness and superciliousness ; when it goes right, the mind is sharpened, the judgment is strengthened, and the heart becomes less selfish. There is nothing specially academic about them, they exist in other places where intelligent youths are allowed to gather together unregimented, but in Cambridge they seem to generate a peculiar clean white light of their own, which can remain serviceable right on into middle age."

## The undergraduate

" passes out into life, bringing with him standards of conduct and memories of affection and beauty which cannot be elsewhere obtained."

## Cambridge is linked in power and grace with ancient Athens.

" The Cephissus flows with the Cam through this city, by the great lawn of King's under the bridge of Clare, towards plane trees which have turned into the chestnuts of Jesus. Ancient and modern unite through the magic of youth."

To keep this view of Cambridge in mind is to understand the angle from which other modes of life are seen. Mr. Forster sees them, as it were, from Cambridge; and from the " exquisite enclosure " of King's, a civilized college where it is obligatory to read for honours, not from the Cambridge which he sums up as " the 'Varsity," and " which takes pass degrees, roars round football fields, sits down in the middle of Hammersmith Broadway after the boat race, and covers actresses with soot." " Silly and idle young men," " hearties and toughs," though he recognizes, with tolerant amusement, their existence, and their part in the fabric of modern Cambridge as in that of ancient Athens, are to him outside

Cambridge in its meaning to him of a mode of life and thought.

> " In its exquisite enclosure [King's] a false idea can be gained of enclosures outside, though not of the infinite verities."

He left the enclosure with a classical degree, a passion for ancient Greece, a passion less reverent and more amused for modern Italy, a profound interest in people, in personal relationships, in modes of life, in life itself; a quick perceptive awareness of individuals; the novelist's gift of taking in, registering, and reproducing the authentic speech and idiom of all sorts of people (take, as small examples of such registering, the conversation of two minor characters, both women—Mrs. Lewin, the pleasant May Week chaperon of *The Longest Journey*, and Madge, the genteel young farmer's wife who offers Margaret refreshment in *Howards End*: there is not a false note in either).

It was obvious that the novelist's was the right form of expression for him. Like Rickie Elliot, he thought he would like to write stories. Greek mythology offered him scope for one side of imagination, the less mature side; through his early articles and short stories move noiselessly those invisible, immortal Greek creatures, dryads, oreads, fauns, Pan, who haunt (or haunted then) the imaginative twilight of the British classic-nurtured mind, though, it is said, few other minds, and least of all the highly practical and day-lit souls of the modern Greek and the modern Italian, both firm realists.

Haunted then. I think this is true. Pan, perhaps gun-shy since the four years of war, has retired from the English scene; the Greeks have slipped into the shades. What young man or woman coming down from Cambridge to-day would permit such intrusions? To-day we are realists; romance (classical or other) stands in a corner, face to the wall, a fool's cap inscribed "Escapist" on her minished head, her visions and her language alike barred from prose, and only permitted in poetry if well disguised. Classical nurture is also at a discount; we are in a practical moment, an urgent, a democratic and a doxical moment, and æsthetic classicism is as much out of mode as the romanticism of the lake-and-mountainy school was then.

But thirty years ago it was different, and the Hellenic and Roman pastoral genii, the kindly or unkindly *turba deorum* who had for four centuries adorned the British landscape, perturbing, disturbing, or merely prettily enturbing it, still flitted on its borders and lurked, derisive, in its leafy brakes.

Individual and epoch: one cannot justly correlate them, it is too difficult, and the individual too unruly. In art, as in other human functions, it is confusing that

*People, less settled than the sliding sand,*
*More mutable than Proteus or the Moon,*
*Turn, and return, in turning of a hand,*
*Like Euripus ebb-flowing every noon.*

Confusing, because of this difficulty it makes in discriminating between the artist's epochless individuality and the period which shapes it. It would be an amusing game to put Mr. Forster back into the 1850's; to transpose him with (say) Thackeray, and to consider a *Pendennis* of 1910, a *Howards End* of 1849. Obviously neither could have been written; but what would have been written instead ? How much of that lightly-stepping, flickering wit, those mystic borderlands, would have emerged out of the solid, sinisterly fascinating, mahogany-and-port Victorian world ? The Wilcox family might have thriven in it; the luckless Bast pair would not have been choked out of life; but the Schlegels ? What kind of a Margaret Schlegel would have moved in it, crinolined, eager, cultivated, candid, a blue-stocking, yet gracious and gay and all for people, all for Life ?

These are idle speculations. As easy to consider how Pope would have written the *Essay on Man* to-day, or Proust his *Swan* when Marivaux was writing *Marianne* and Fielding *Tom Jones*. It would be entertaining, but much too troublesome, and there is probably no satisfactory answer. Better to take writers and their backgrounds as we find them.

We find Mr. Forster and his contemporaries just stepped out of one tremendous century into another, their backs to that rather hectic and uneasy period of their childhood, the eighteen-nineties, which they did not know (being too young to judge for themselves, and too early in time to have heard the judgments which future critics were to formulate) were decadent, "yellow," even " naughty." Scepticism about all such period labels is generally sound, and not difficult of attainment. Things happen; individuals function; the arts make whatever particular flourish is indicated by the genius of the few or dictated by fashion to the many; the crazy pattern thrown by chance together is later fitted by impatient and generalizing minds into a jigsaw whole, the recalcitrant bits being lopped and hacked away and thrown into corners so that they may not spoil the picture. There is no need to believe anything about any period, except that certain things happened in it and certain individuals functioned; which, if you come to think of it, is more than enough.

Still, if one wants to, one may easily believe that the nineteenth century died in Great Britain in a fit of vaunting and buccaneering hubris, rather like that of the swaggering Elizabethans who supposed that the New World and its riches would all be theirs quite soon, but adding to this delirium the full-fed pleasure of achievement, the

B

child's delight in imperial possessions so much showier than anything the other children had.

*All thine shall be the subject main,*
*And every shore it circles thine.*

Age-old ambition; the realization of even a fraction of it inebriates and giddies. It gives, too, an uneasy qualm; a pinch of appeasing incense is thrown over the shoulder, as it were, with a chanted " Lest we forget," at those gods who lie in wait to destroy those whom they have first made mad, and who ultimately founder all empires.

One reaction to all this rather noisy, puffy and enfevered pomp was the sharpening of the guerilla warfare that is perpetually waged between society and the individual. The literature of the eighteen-nineties and the early nineteen-hundreds in Europe continually waves this banner. Traditional ethical standards, " *les formules et les préjuges héréditaires*," are even more than usually in a state of flux, and the closer cult of oneself, said Maurice Barrès, " *finira bien par dégager d'elle-même une morale et des devoirs nouveaux*." The tautened subjective alertness of the short story of the nineties, both in France and in England, drove through mass conventionalism like a sharp flavour; individual sensation and awareness of life found more and more this release. Novelists, compelled by those exigencies of the inscrutable laws of publishing which dictate their destinies,

had been induced to compress such thoughts and
narrations as they conceived into smaller compass,
and to express themselves in what their forbears
of the 'seventies and 'eighties would have regarded
as long-short stories. No more three-deckers; no
more *Vanity Fairs*, *Daniel Derondas*, nor *Egoists*
were to be permitted, until the magniloquence of
these modern days was to encourage immensity
once more. *Jean-Christophe*, begun in 1904, had
to be published as a cycle, like the Arthurian and
Alexandrian cycles of the Middle Ages. Mr.
Forster arrived as a story-writer into a world
twinkling with the earlier coruscations of H. G.
Wells, ruddy with the sinking but still flashing
imperial torch of Mr. Kipling, sturdily muscled,
manned and midlandized by Enoch Arnold
Bennett, decorated by the elegant gaieties of Max
Beerbohm, Saki, Henry Harland, Anatole France,
and the left-overs from the *Yellow Book* and the
*Savoy*, entertained by the Benson family, sustained
by Hardy, James and Meredith as its grand old
men, interested in the experiments of Mallarmé
and Gide, excited by Huysmans, wearying of Zola
and naturalism, of Pierre Loti and romance, of
Paul Bourget and religiousness, just awakening to
the Russian excitement of the uneventful hour, yet
still rich in plots and passions, with windows that
open every now and then on to some uncanny land of
ghosts, centaurs or magic. There was a rich and exciting choice of field for the young rider into fiction.

# CHAPTER II

MOST of us, whatever we may do about it later, write poetry in our twenties: such an activity is, at the least or at the most (as the case may be) a vent for our subliminal selves; into it we discharge our ghost-consciousness. E. M. Forster vented and discharged his otherwise; mainly in that most ancient and most continuous form of literature, the short story, which in his hands had usually a back door opening on to intangible worlds. Into many of his short early sketches flit those seducing shades, those " extra persons," who give their eerie, their faintly sinister twist to the destinies of those present. They even invade the world of tourism. There is, for example, an enchanting account, dated 1904, of a visit to the small Greek port of Cnidus.* The Hellenic travellers, including Mr. Forster, land at Cnidus on a dark and rainy evening; they stumble about among mud and masonry; they see, imperfectly, temples, a theatre, the Trireme harbour;

---

* Reprinted in *Abinger Harvest*, a collection of about sixty articles of various periods, published 1936. When I have mentioned an essay reprinted in this volume, I have marked it *Abinger Harvest*.

they return to their boats in the rain: but, whereas twenty-one have set out, twenty-two return.

" Someone had joined us. It is well known (is it not ?) who that extra person always is. This time he came hurrying down to the beach at the last moment, and tried to peer into our faces. I could hardly see his ; but it was young, and it did not look unkind. He made no answer to our tremulous greetings, but raised his hand to his head and then laid it across his breast, meaning, I understand, that his brain and his heart were ours. Everyone made clumsy imitations of his gesture to keep him in a good temper. His manners were perfect. I am not sure that he did not offer to lift people into the boats. But there was a general tendency to avoid his attentions, and we put off in an incredibly short space of time. He melted away in the darkness. . . ."

No doubt, a Greek fisherman. But Greek (and Latin) fishermen, peasants, and even cab-drivers, have, when Mr. Forster encounters them, an unrestrainable tendency to hint at being something else, something odder, more primeval, strays from a pagan world. Even Stephen Wonham, the young Wiltshire yeoman's son of *The Longest Journey*, is seen by sophisticates as such a pagan stray.

" Certain figures of the Greeks, to whom we continually return, suggested him a little. One expected nothing of him— no purity of phrase nor swift-edged thought. Yet the conviction grew that he had been back somewhere—back to some table of the gods, spread in a field where there is no noise, and that he belonged for ever to the guests with whom he had eaten."

One is uncertain whether to call this consciousness of a Greek pagan fringe to the modern world native or acquired.

> " That evening, under those weeping clouds, the imagination became creative, taking wings because there was nothing to bid it rise, flying impertinently against all archæology and sense, uttering bird-like cries of ' Greek ! Greek ! ' as it flew, declaring that it heard voices because all was so silent, and saw faces because it was too dark to see."

Imagination cried " Greek! Greek! " to him not only at Cnidus, but in the English countryside, in Italy, all over the place. This passed. But what was fundamental in it remained: the mysticism through which he sees people as transcending themselves, as symbols, each surrounded by the aura of some strange other world in which his or her true being walks, while the being's phenomenal self amusingly, agreeably, or deplorably gestures on the revealed stage before the dropped curtain. Mrs. Wilcox, the mistress of Howards End, for instance, was a nice, quiet, ungifted elderly lady; as with Stephen Wonham, one neither expected from her nor got purity of phrase or swift-edged thought. " Yet the conviction grew "—that she had been back somewhere. Back where ? Well, in the case of Mrs. Wilcox, I am not quite sure, though Mr. Forster possibly is. Margaret Schlegel felt her great; Mr. Forster felt her great; I feel, and have always felt, that they may be wrong, that, led by the

will-o'-the-wisp light of enlarging fancy, they
are lending to a nice, unselfish, honest-minded,
country-loving, but fairly ordinary person some
aura which belongs really to their own greater
awareness of what she and her kind might
stand for, some perceptiveness which is rather
theirs than hers. It does not matter; it comes to
the same thing, or pretty nearly. The artist's perceptiveness cuts through wrappings and veils to
lay bare the human being within them, and,
having perceived this, does on it some carving,
chiselling and moulding, according to his notions
of what it must surely be. All artists do this.
Mr. Forster, with his sharp sense of what ought
to be, of what makes life ironic, tragic, comic,
good or base, of personal relationships and values
as they not only phenomenally but noumenally
exist, is an expert at the job.

He would agree, one supposes, with Anatole
France, that Irony and Pity should be the witnesses and the judges of human life.

" Plus je songe à la vie humaine, plus je crois qu'il faut lui
donner par témoins et pour juges l'Ironie et la Pitié, comme
les Egyptiens appelaient sur leurs morts la déesse Isis et la
déesse Nephtys. L'Ironie et la Pitié sont deux bonnes
conseillières ; l'une, en souriant, nous rend la vie aimable ;
l'autre, qui pleurt, nous la rend sacrée. L'Ironie que j'invoque
n'est point cruelle. Elle ne raille ni l'Amour ni la beauté.
Elle est douce et bienveillante. Son rire calme la colère, et
c'est elle qui nous enseigne à nous moquer des méchants et des
sots que nous pouvions, sans elle, avoir la faiblesse de haïr."

Most novelists and dramatists might subscribe in theory to this. But for Mr. Forster, more than for M. Bergeret, the two goddesses are always on duty together, joining hands, holding candles to illustrate with their elfish flickering the misty corners of personality. (The misty corners are, of course, Mr. Forster's only, M. Bergeret knowing nothing of these.) They are not only witnesses and judges but artists; they wreathe the misty corners and borders into new shapes, they throw auras of who knows what round the forms on which they ironically and compassionately gaze; they take untidy, sprawling, humourless, unpitiable, indigestible lives and destinies into their hands and pattern them to their liking. They give them style, charm, rhythm, grace; they create a reality more real than actuality, a quality of life more alive than life itself; in brief, they behave like artists.

What was so remarkable was that Mr. Forster successfully commanded their services at an age when most writers have not yet learnt to use them. Here is an essay of 1903, written a year after leaving Cambridge: it is called *Macolnia Shops*,* and it is about a Greek bronze toilet case engraved with figures, in the Kirchner Museum in Rome, and about Dindia Macolnia, the Roman lady who went shopping for it and gave it as a present to her daughter. In this exquisite brief essay you will find all the charm, the humour, the

* *Abinger Harvest.*

gay, gentle, mocking flexibility of rhythm, almost every characteristic turn of style, that you will find in essays on Jane Austen and Hannah More thirty years later. That is odd and unusual. Most of us experiment, begin clumsily, blunder and tumble leggily about like young colts, beat out our style little by little. Mr. Forster seems to have slipped into his early, as into a suit made for him. It grew and developed, but has not really changed very much. He was fonder then than now of routing in the odd corners of classical and medieval history; since then the eighteenth and nineteenth centuries have captured his humour and his fancy, and the twentieth his attention. Thirty odd years back he was writing of Dindia Macolnia, of Gemistus Pletho, of Girolamo Cardan, with the same pretty irony and sympathetic wit. The sentences surprise laughter. Gemistus Pletho, " wrote a tract *Concerning the difference between Plato and Aristotle.*\* Hitherto it had not been known that there was any difference; and as the Church's philosophy was based on Aristotle, a conflict began which divided the learned world for some fifty years." It is the kind of gay and airy shorthand that other writers have used, but none more gracefully. (" Three centuries," however, would have sounded more effective than " fifty years," and have been truer.) One difference between Mr. Forster and others who have

\* *Abinger Harvest.*

used something of the same mode is that his
historical characters—Pletho and his eager fellow
controversialists, and all the rest of them—please
us and please him. He is fond of them; he likes
the polite and earnest Platonist; he is even fond
of Cardan,* whom some have greatly distasted (I
have heard an Italian professor call him " quel
porchino "), others despised, many forgotten that
he ever lived, which was the one posthumous
fate he dreaded. This ironic affection for the
characters of history, fed by writing of them, is
infectious; the reader catches it. There are some
(not very many) persons in his novels whom Mr.
Forster thoroughly dislikes; few in his essays on
actual people, living or dead. He finds them—or,
anyhow, leaves them—amiable and endearing
oddities, to be cherished, quizzed and esteemed.
It is more than a pity that he has not found time,
and probably will not, to write a brief history of
the world; it would make not only for illumination and entertainment, but for a greater phil-
anthropy, a livelier sympathy with our so peculiar,
so lamentable, so often detestable, yet so admirable
human tale. His teratology is of the pleased,
appreciating order, and he is delighted with our
curious zoo.

His inquisitive pleasure in it turned him, one
supposes, to story-writing about it. There is
extant a considerable part of an early unpublished

* *Abinger Harvest.*

novel, written at about twenty years of age: it is about middle-class snobs, who despised the vulgar; it is about views; it is about a minor public school and its barbaric standards; it is about a delicate and missish boy and his friendship with a common young schoolmaster next door, who committed, as did his mother, every solecism, and was despised by the boy's snob aunt. One sees in it the embryo of *A Room with a View*; also of Sawston School, which comes into *The Longest Journey*. Snobbery and views (the views that are looked at, not held)—these, paired as antitheses, seen as good and evil, haunted Mr. Forster's mind, even in boyhood. Edgar, the delicate, clever boy, is the battle-ground of these antagonists. The stage is set for the same battle—call it between reality and humbug, nature and cant—that is to sound through all his pre-war novels. This early fragment is, of course, callow; it is a try-out only. But it is fun, it shows a comic sense, a sense of words, a sense of people. It opens thus:

" ' They are Nottingham lace ! '

" Mrs. Manchett turned from the window with a compressed face. Edgar gathered the purport of his aunt's words, though he did not grasp their exact meaning. She proceeded to commentate.

" ' From the moment that rosewood chair—you remember —came out of the van, I guessed the kind of people they would be. Then there was the dreadful malachite clock and the two blue vases and the two little girls with their hair done in a most common style. Then the son carried the mattress in himself—most nice and kind ; I am not saying it tells against him a bit—but it all shows.  And now here are the curtains —Nottingham lace.  Come and look.' "

A few years later, Mr. Forster would have made Mrs. Manchett, Edgar, and the vulgarians next door, more attractive.  Here they are rough sketches, too definite, simple and flat; they live too coarsely, thinly and typically, but they do live.

In technique, there is a long gap between this novel about the Nottingham lace curtains (had it ever a name ?) and the short stories which the author, three or four years later, was writing and sending to magazines.  These were largely the kind of stories which Rickie Elliot describes to Agnes Pembroke:

" ' What I write is too silly.  It can't happen.  For instance, a stupid vulgar man is engaged to a lovely young lady.  He wants her to live in the house, but she only cares for woods. She shocks him this way and that, but gradually he tames her, and makes her nearly as dull as he is.  One day she has a last explosion—over the snobby wedding presents—and flies out of the drawing-room window, shouting ' Freedom and truth ! ' Near the house is a little dell full of fir-trees, and she runs into it.  He comes there the next moment.  But she's gone.'

" ' Awfully exciting.  Where ? '

" ' Oh Lord, she's a dryad ! '" cried Rickie in great disgust. ' She's turned into a tree.'

" ' Rickie, it's very good indeed.  That kind of thing has something in it.  Of course you get it all through Greek and Latin.  How upset the man must be when he sees the girl turn.'

" ' He doesn't see her. He never guesses. Such a man could never see a dryad.'

" ' So you describe how she turns just before he comes up ? '

" ' No. Indeed, I don't ever say that she does turn. I don't use the word dryad once.'

" ' I think you ought to put that part plainly. Otherwise, with such an original story, people might miss the point. Have you had any luck with it ? '

" ' Magazines ? I haven't tried. . . . I've got quite a pile of little stories all harping on this ridiculous idea of getting into touch with Nature.'

" ' I wish you weren't so modest. It's simply splendid as an idea.' "

Later on, Rickie tries to get his stories published. He " hoped they would make a book, and that the book might be called *Pan Pipes*." But editors sent them back. " Your story does not convince," said one of them. " See life, Mr. Elliot, and then send us another story."

Mr. Forster's own early stories were mostly collected much later in *The Celestial Omnibus* and *The Eternal Moment*. Many of them were first printed in the *Independent Review* and elsewhere; some, like Rickie's, must have come back to him with civil notes. It is the fact, and one must face it, that many of them were about getting into touch with Nature. In one, a curate gets into touch with a Wiltshire faun, and is saved thereby from himself. From being an odious, facetious and idiotic curate, one gathers, though we have only his word for it, that he becomes a happy, genuine and honest one. That kind of thing, as

Agnes remarked, has something in it; but as it stands it tantalizes, because one would like to see the curate's transformation, not merely to be told by him (probably not a good judge) that it has occurred. In *Other Kingdom*, which is, if not the best of these stories, the longest, fullest and most attractive, a young woman escapes from her pretentious humbug of a lover into a beech copse and turns into a beech tree. All the same, it is a brilliant, charming and witty story; the usual conflict, Reality against Sham, embroidered with amusing human detail. As usual, the happy savage escapes from and defeats the cultured snob. The dendrofied young woman, the happy savage introduced to civilization, is one of Mr. Forster's most engaging heroines. *The Story of a Panic* is less sophisticated and more obviously mystical; Pan breaks into a conventional English picnic party on an Italian hill-side and takes possession of a boy. Again the primitive, the nature-possessed, escapes from the conventional friends who strive to hold him. So, too, in *Albergo Empedocle* (not reprinted) the simple and un-æsthetic young man, despised by the cultured young woman to whom he is engaged, escapes into a remembered pre-existence in Greek Sicily, is disbelieved by his friends, and shut up for mad. *The Celestial Omnibus* is about a child's journey in a dream omnibus to a dream world; here the child, the genuine liver of poetry, takes naturally

to a glory that fills the literary and poetic adult
with terror and kills him. In *The Road from
Colonnus* it is, for once, convention, dullness and
Britain which defeat adventurous living, adventurous death, and Greece. *The Eternal Moment*
too is a tale of partial defeat; the defeat of a vivid
moment in a woman's past by the common and
ignominious present; yet of victory too, the
victory of integrity, candour and middle-age over
ignominy. Miss Raby, the middle-aged novelist,
is something like Margaret Schlegel grown older;
the same frank disregard of appearances and
generous, startling candour. It is a remarkable
story; perhaps the most remarkable of all; regarded merely as a tour-de-force it is notable; as
a tragi-comedy it is brilliant. Taken alone, it
would show that by the end of 1904, when it was
written, Mr. Forster was already a highly accomplished artist.

The other stories of that period are cruder and
more mystical than this. There is *The Machine
Stops*, which shows fertile and graphic Wellsian
inventiveness combined with Chestertonian mech-
anophobia; in manner and matter it is the least
Forsterian of his writings. It has a Forster moral,
but lacks charm, humour and style; it might have
been written by someone else. Not so the *Story
of the Siren*, which opens, " Few things have been
more beautiful than my notebook on the Deist
Controversy as it fell downward through the

waters of the Mediterranean." A boatman begins to remove his clothes to dive for it. " Thank him, dear," said my aunt; " that is to say, tell him he is very kind, but perhaps another time."

The boatman, a child of nature, dives, returns the Deist Controversy, and relates to its author the story of how his brother had once seen the Siren and had gone mad, had married a girl who had also seen her, and who had been pushed over a cliff by a priest when about to bear a child because the child, if born, would bring the Siren out of the sea to sing on the earth, and then the Church would be destroyed and the world changed. In this story, odd and sad and lovely, paganism and joy go under and conventionalism for the time remains on top. In the brief and gay girls'-school story, *Co-ordination*, it is the other way round; joy wins and the school System goes under. And in *The Other Side of the Hedge* neither side wins; we are shown the dusty road on which men and women march, dogged and unresting, towards some unknown goal, and, contrasted, the idle, lovely spaces of country on the hedge's other side, where men and women who have abandoned the feverish race live in peace and in the moment, enjoying " the magic song of nightingales and the odour of invisible hay, and stars piercing the fading sky." It is a comment on the futility of progress, the illusion of advance; the moral is *carpe diem*. The country

beyond the hedge has been written of by poets
from other angles; Vaughan's, for instance:

> If thou canst get but hither,
>     There grows the flower of peace,
> The Rose that cannot wither,
>     Thy fortress and thy ease.
>     Leave then thy foolish ranges. . . .

But Mr. Forster's country was the pagan's—
the pagan's, that is, as traditionally understood, for
the pagans of history have had, often, a hearty
belief in worldly progress and strenuous activity.

Looking through the stories, one finds them
nearly all to be abstract and brief chronicles of the
earlier novels. In them Reality, Life, Truth,
Passion, Gaiety, Nature, Youth, call the thing
what you will, fights for its life, in various garbs
and with various weapons, against Unreality,
Death, Sham, Conventionalism, Dullness, Pomp-
ousness, Age. Mr. Forster had a message, and
the message was about this eternal battle, in which
victory ebbed and flowed now to one side now to
the other. All life gave him news of the battle.
Music gave it to him, as Beethoven gave it to
Helen Schlegel.

" The music started with a goblin walking quietly over the
universe, from end to end. Others followed him. They were
not aggressive creatures ; it was that that made them so
terrible to Helen. They merely observed in passing that there
was no such thing as splendour or heroism in the world. . . .

" Beethoven chose to make it all right in the end. He built

C

the ramparts up. He blew with his mouth for the second time, and again the goblins were scattered. He brought back the gusts of splendour, the heroism, the youth, the magnificence of life and of death, and, amid vast roarings of a superhuman joy, he led his Fifth Symphony to its conclusion. But the goblins were there. They could return."

The banners, the goblins, the drums, sound through all the stories, and through the two novels that he began about the same time. But the mystical element, which is in the open in the stories, often magic and supernatural, runs more obscurely through the novels, a thread inter- woven with ordinary life, ordinary people, un- helped by deities, fauns, dendro-metamorphoses, or other mythological aids to a fuller life. The people in the novels have to grope their own un- aided way to this life; some have it, others lay their hands on it, others have to struggle through dark- ness and bewilderment towards it; others, again, know it not, and, we are given to understand, never can: the doors of life are shut to them, they have shut them themselves. But not even Stephen, the pagan of the Wiltshire downs, is allowed to be openly a faun, though at moments he gets pretty near it, and one looks now and then rather anxiously at his ears.

# CHAPTER III

THERE has always been recognized a pleasant amorous disease to which the English are peculiarly susceptible: falling in love with Italy. It would appear to have been prevalent since the early Middle Ages, and has been by many testy and sardonic writers deplored, as making English travellers who had tripped to the continent sillier and even more vicious than they had been before. Even the patriotic and race-proud John Milton contracted it. Indeed, few of our island race have been immune, until recent years, when Fascism, Signor Mussolini, Abyssinia, the Spanish invasion, Italian broadcast views on Britain, and other of those unfortunate disasters which tarnish international affections, have turned this xenophily rather into an achievement, like the love of God, than the spontaneous liking of people for their charm which is what the English used to feel for the Italians.

Mr. Forster, residing for a time in Italy in more felicitous days than these, fell deeply in love with it and with its denizens, with this enchanting, unaffected, cynical, callous, gay and somewhat barbaric Latin people, whose very humbug is emitted with a glorious gesture of eloquent absurdity, so different from the stiff, stilted, half-muted humbug of the fog-bound and inhibited British. From this amour proceeded two novels, *Where Angels Fear to Tread*, and *A Room with a View*. The second of these was not published until 1908, after *The Longest Journey*. But its embryo was conceived several years earlier, and the draft of its first part is still extant, younger and less good than the published book, with more narrative explanation of what is in the later version revealed more sharply and amusingly by talk; its characters have not yet decided how to put themselves across. There is more and wordier description; the opening sentences have a flavour of Jane Austen. Still, there, in essence, it is; the same people and the same plot, and much of the same manner and words. Perhaps the author did not know how he would finish it; perhaps another story haunted him; anyhow, for one reason or another he laid it aside for three years, and instead of going on with it wrote *Rescue* (later called *Monteriano*, later still *Where Angels Fear to Tread*). As has been indicated, it is the novel of a young man deeply, though not uncritically, in love with the Italian race, Italian civilization, the Italian angle of life. The young Italian, Gino, is a vulgar and mercenary youth who ill-treats his wife; he is a barbarian. His creator modifies nothing of this, conceals nothing, idealizes nothing. Gino is, in many of his aspects, disgusting. He would probably to-day be a brutal young Fascist. But Mr. Forster, his antithesis, the product of a sensitive and humane liberal and Cambridge culture, loves Gino, the tough, flashy, extrovert Latin youth, the kind of youth whom one meets now and then in Juvenal or Petronius, handsome, avaricious, greedy and stupid, something of a smart Alec, something of a crook, more of a spoilt child, his black hair oiled, his body poised magnificently against the magnificent Tuscan landscape, against the magnificent, brutal centuries of Roman culture. What English creatures can help loving Gino ? Not Mr. Forster, not his readers, not the prigs from Sawston who had come out to hate him. For this is the story of the conquest of commonplace suburban English respectability by Italian charm, by cheerful, graceful and rather brutal paganism. And a very good story, even merely as story, it is. It is not always enough noticed that Mr. Forster is one of our best plot-makers; his novels always tell a story, and always a dramatic story; they are first-class theatre stuff, in which an exciting time is had by all, and are passionately readable. " The novel tells a story," he says, and goes on to wish that it were not so, that it could be, instead, " melody, or perception of the truth, not this low atavistic form." But one cannot believe that he wishes this

more than occasionally; or, anyhow, that he used
to wish it when he was writing the things. Tell
stories he must and would: stories about people,
stories about gods, fauns and sirens, stories about
clashes, conflicts, antagonisms, lives, deaths,
lovers, friends, aunts, clergymen, old ladies,
Italians, young women and young men. The
melody, the perception of the truth, streams
through the low atavistic form, but (fortunately)
does not attempt to supersede it. It is, in fact, the
form that matters most; the melody, the truth
and the perception are important, but what matters
most vitally in the novels is not the soul but the
body. What makes *Where Angels Fear to Tread*
brilliant and delightful is the comedy and tragedy
of those two vulgar innocents, those two gay
children of nature, English Lilia and Italian Gino,
of smug and cultivated Philip Herriton, foolish
(I fear incredible) Caroline Abbott, disagreeable
(I hope incredible) Harriet, sly, managing, all
too credible Mrs. Herriton, and the background
of the small Italian town, where life is conducted
in the caffé, the farmacia, and the piazza. It is an
amazing book for a quite young man to have conceived and written; more amazing, though a less
good and rich novel, than *The Longest Journey*,
which followed it, for *The Longest Journey* is
largely built out of experience, it is about lives
more similar in structure and background, though
not in circumstance, to the lives the writer knew,

but this first odd and pleasant invention is about
lives he could scarcely have known except
remotely, and yet they emerge solid and round.
Such beings as Gino and his friends one sees talking together in the piazza outside the farmacia;
one does not really know them.   Such as Lilia one
may see (if one is fortunate) sprawling about a
morning-coffee shop, laughing and chaffing at a
cinema, gaping cheerfully and vacantly at shop
windows, but one does not really know Lilia
either, one has, as a rule, no such luck.   Mr.
Forster cannot really have known well either of
these merry and touching extroverts from an
uncultivated stratum of alien social life; yet how,
in his hands, they bounce with the life he imparts,
jig authentically to his sardonically authentic
tunes.   They assault the senses like a rank, full-
flavoured, common wine, a cheap, vulgar scent,
a jigging Naples or cockney tune.   Their relationship and their dialogue is superb (though in what
language, since Gino spoke little English and
Lilia less Italian, was it conducted ?   But it does
not matter).   Even better are the conversations
between the Italians.   Gino's friend from Chiasso
enquires about his marriage :

" ' But tell me more.  She is English.  That is good, very
good.  An English wife is very good indeed.  And she is
rich ? '
" ' Immensely rich.'
" ' Blonde or dark ? '

" ' Blonde.'

" ' Is it possible ? '

" ' It pleases me very much,' said Gino simply.   ' If you remember, I always desired a blonde.' Three or four men had collected, and were listening.

" ' We all desire one,' said Spiridione.  ' But you, Gino, deserve your good fortune, for you are a good son, a brave man, and a true friend, and from the very first moment I saw you I wished you well.'

" ' No compliments, I beg,' said Gino, standing with his hands crossed on his chest and a smile of pleasure on his face.

" Spiridione addressed the other men, none of whom he had ever seen before.  ' Is it not true ?  Does not he deserve this wealthy blonde ? '

" ' He does deserve her,' said all the men."

Translate this into Italian, and see how right it reads.  There are moments when Gino seems to me the best thing that Mr. Forster has ever done, in spite of the melodrama inherent in his conception.  He is a radiant cad and bragster.  The scene at the Monteriano opera house is magnificent farce;  that between Gino and Philip after the baby's death is blood-and-thunder tragic stuff that twangs sharply at the nerves;  it has for a time a Senecan kind of sensationalism that the Elizabethans might have envied;  but they would have despised it in the end, for no blood is spilt, and the agonists, parted and reconciled by a woman, end drinking milk together.  I like this scene, and the concise, abrupt, moved manner of its telling;  I am stirred by Gino's anguish and Philip's, and can even accept the apotheosis of

Miss Abbott. The last paragraph of the chapter is one of those simple assaults on the emotions that were more used thirty years ago than now.

> " He drank the milk, and then, either by accident or in some spasm of pain, broke the jug to pieces. Perfetta exclaimed in bewilderment. ' It does not matter,' he told her. ' It does not matter. It will never be wanted any more.' "

The whole book belongs to a young and emotional world, the world of a young man at the beginning of the twentieth century who has just left the University and fallen in love with Italy. It could not be written to-day, for a hundred reasons. A minor one is that young men do not now fall in love with Italy; they fall in love—if love is the word—with Spain, or with Mexico, or with Russia, or with Portugal, or with Ecuador; lands more savage, fierce, tortured and mysterious, lands it is impossible to pet. Nor would Gino, with his merry braggadocio, be a likely figure in the more tortured and arid modern landscape; he would be more sensual, nasty and brutish, we should hear more of his lusts and amours, and he would probably have gouged out Philip's eyes instead of merely hurting his arm. There would be more blood and less milk, and the Elizabethan Senecans would have preferred it. Philip himself would be different; less of a prig, less bloodless, more compact of parts and passions, and therefore less amusing. Miss Abbott, a girl of twenty-three, remains " Miss Abbott " throughout the book, not only to Philip, who had known her all their lives and lived in the same place, but to Mr. Forster and us: he is as delightfully prim and distant with her as Miss Austen is with her gentlemen. In the last pages, Philip, now in love with her, almost tells her so; she breaks down and sobs and tells him she loves Gino; but still they are Miss Abbott and Mr. Herriton; not Mr. Darcy and Miss Elizabeth Bennett themselves could have been more prettily proper.

There could, of course, be no Miss Abbott in a novel of to-day; a modern Caroline, loving Gino, would have had him, if only for a time; she might have ended by having Philip, too; in any case the scene in which she drops her pride and reticence with so much effort and tells him of her hidden, and in her eyes degrading, passion is unthinkable in a novel written since the war. A new kind of young woman has got into our novels, uninhibited, philandrous, high-geared, for ever in and out of bed. Mr. Forster has never used her, and, I imagine, could not; she is off his beat. Most of his young women, and most of his men, are virginal, inhibited, thinking beings, more interested in the psychological than the physical aspects of love. If the exigencies of truth convinced him, as a conscientious artist, that he must bed two lovers, he would do so, but I think that he would be both bored and embarrassed by the banal and

indelicate situation in which they would find
themselves, and would inform us of it in a few
brief, sudden and chilly words; the incident
would have no charms for him. When it occurs
in *Howards End* (a unique occasion in his novels)
he omits to inform us until some months have
elapsed and Helen is about to bear a child; and
even then neither he nor we entirely, I think,
believe it. Indeed, in 1910 this was still thought
peculiar behaviour on the part of well-brought-up
young ladies. The question is, what would Mr.
Forster do with his young women and young men
should he write, as we all hope, another novel
now ? Nothing, we may be sure, that we expect.

He draws women—women of the upper classes
living in twentieth-century pre-war England—
with a more than feminine insight and deftness.
But Caroline Abbott is a rather raw and juvenile
sketch, before he got his hand in; she is still what
his later women are not, something of a man's
woman, seen uncertainly from without. Prim
and commonplace, if at times odd, she suddenly
shoots up into larger than life-size, she becomes
a heroine, a goddess, a sybil, controlling destinies.
She loves greatly and nobly; but love she does,
one believes it, it is true. She has a strong and
no doubt fleeting infatuation, that she believes
will never leave her. "For, as far as she knew
anything about herself, she knew that her
passions once aroused, were sure." Of course at

twenty-three she believes that. Possibly Mr. Forster, being not so much more himself, believed it too.

Philip's sudden love, on the other hand, is a tepid, hearsay, and singularly unconvincing affair: one is offered no evidence that Philip knew what love was. But sexual love, though it is the pivot of one of his novels, never concerns or interests Mr. Forster much in itself. The only love in *Where Angels Fear to Tread* that moves him or us to much conviction is Gino's for his baby. The other loves are, by comparison, childish, invented and unreal; but this supplies passion and tragedy of a quality to balance the ironic comedy of the rest.

Reviews are notoriously odd. They seldom make such acute criticisms of books as intelligent readers who do not review. *Where Angels Fear to Tread* was praised highly by C. F. G. Masterman in the *Nation*, and by Edward Garnett in the *Speaker*. But the *Spectator* said it was " painful " (a singular word, in greater favour with reviewers once than now) and found the characters abnormal, adding, however, that the author " deals with the subject in a manner devoid of offence," which suggests that the reviewer found the kidnapping of a baby from its Italian father in some way indelicate. On the whole, the book had an excellent press. But on the whole, also, a rather stupid press. No reviewer, that is, pointed out that Harriet was a little too bad to be true and jarred with the texture of the rest of the book; that the ironic tragedy of Gino and Lilia was as brilliantly funny and sad as it in fact is; or (much more important) that here was a new wit, awareness and grace arrived among novelists; I am not sure that anyone even said that Mr. Forster must be watched, though it is difficult to believe that they all avoided this.  But it was a good press, and we may take it that thereafter he *was* watched (whatever this flattering and embarrassing process may entail; about most of us the command that we should be watched has from time to time in our early careers gone from kindly critics forth, but whether or not anyone obeyed it, we never knew).

# CHAPTER IV

## THE LONGEST JOURNEY

CHRONOLOGICALLY, the next book to mention is the Temple Classics edition of the *Æneid*, with English verse translation by E. Fairfax Taylor and notes and introduction by E. M. Forster, published in 1906. It is a nice introduction. Mr. Forster, like most of us, found the *Æneid* rather unsatisfactory, better in parts than as a whole; Virgil " loves most the things that profess to matter least, a simile rather than the action that it illustrates, a city full of apple trees rather than the soldiers who march out of it " —and as a heroic epic it fails. The pious Æneas is something of a bore, and an unconvincing bore at that, and treats Dido abominably. Virgil's attitude to life is briefly analysed, and his literary position prettily summed. There is here and there a worn phrase to remind us of the difficulty of treading with *esprit* in such a trodden track, and Mr. Forster's most characteristic graces look out only rarely, like pools between the unwatered reaches of a river bed; it is, in fact, a scholarly and intelligent introduction, but only occasionally in the authentic voice of the author of that engaging fragment of Roman speculation, *Macolnia Shops*, or the later and still more agreeable *Pharos and Pharillon*. The pious Æneas and his poet are a rather weighty burden to shoulder, and particularly in a Temple Classic, where you may not treat them just as you might like. But the last sentences are characteristic:

> " At the present day, in spite of much vague menace, he still stands firm. People will always declare that he is not like Homer, but the assertion is as harmless as it is accurate. He is more in danger from his friends, for we are too apt to read our own thoughts into him, and our thoughts are too often second-rate. Let us not equip him with any scheme. Above all, let us not make him too tearful or too mellow, for that is the direction in which modern eulogy, following the example of Tennyson, would seem to tend."

The historical notes are adequate, if necessarily brief.

Meanwhile, *The Longest Journey* (published 1907) was in writing.

This is at once the most personal and the most universal of the five novels; and obviously the most autobiographical. It is about Cambridge, and Tonbridge school, and Wiltshire, and Rickie Elliot, who wrote little stories and got married by mistake. It is about friendship, the good and happy life among friends, and the bad and unhappy in the alien world of shams. It is about a dreary marriage with a dreadful woman, a dreary life of teaching in a dreadful school; it is about shades of the prison house, about a long dark tunnel into which a man enters from freedom, and at last struggles into freedom again for a moment, to die in darkness at the end. It is, in fact, about Life, as it appears to the frightened and sensitive young. It is bitter and passionate, emotional and idealistic, exalted and frightening and afraid; the book of a man afraid of the tunnel; he has not been into it himself, except perhaps in boyhood, but has imagined it, like a nightmare. All the middle part of the book, the part called " Sawston," has the texture of nightmare; it is dreadful with the dreadfulness of the dark wood in which one gropes lost as a child, lost for ever, with the remembered daylight behind, the daylight and the friends that one will not see again. Reading it, the sensitive young identify their lives with Rickie's; they, too, are in the dark wood, going the dreariest and the longest journey chained to some dreadful companion, some sorrowful tedious life, they are for ever damned.

This section of the book has the unrelieved horror that only nightmare can have; had it been written out of actual personal experience of a dreary marriage, it must have been less vivid, the issues more confused, the sadness snarled and flattened with all kinds of the incongruous, and some of the mitigating, facts which make daily life. As it stands, it is the abyss of night into which one dreads to fall, a dark miasma of dank and stifling mists: *malorum immensa vorago et gurges*, the whirlpool waiting to suck one under, the hell of lost souls.

For its writer believed in lost souls. I have heard him called a Manichean, who foredooms his characters to salvation or perdition, and the comment has some colour of truth, but it is not true, for he believes in struggle and recovery. Rickie, married and established at Sawston school (the same Sawston, one assumes, that was the drab and soulless haunt of the Herritons and Miss Abbott, and was so different from Monteriano—or did Mr. Forster use the name merely as a symbol, as one might say Inferno, Gomorrah or Wigan ?—Rickie, here established, began to join the lost souls. " He remained conscientious and decent, but the spiritual part of him proceeded towards ruin." It is this deterioration of Rickie, more than his misery, that gives the nightmare quality. The spiritual part of him proceeded towards ruin; could any fate be more desolating ? It all but got there. The same degradation, defilement and annulment of the spirit is expressed in *Howards End* by the sneering goblins of Beethoven's Fifth Symphony, walking quietly over the universe from end to end, observing that there was no such thing as splendour or heroism in the world. " Helen could not contradict them, for once at all events she had felt the same, and had seen the reliable walls of youth collapse.

D

Panic and emptiness! Panic and emptiness! The goblins were right."

The walls of youth had collapsed long before Rickie's marriage and life at Sawston; they collapsed when he left Cambridge. Cambridge was the good life, the way of truth and salvation, outside it lay an alien world of false gods, of shoddy and sham, full of people not serious and not truthful. Cambridge was Eden, from whence, if one made the wrong choice, ate from the wrong tree, one's spirit was expelled with flaming swords, to wander lost and half alive in the barren lands beyond, those dim lands where, as Virgil told Dante of its colourless shades, " la sconoscente vita, che i fe' sozzi, ad ogni conoscenza or li fa bruni "—the unperceiving life that soiled them, now makes them too dim for any recognition.

Rickie, leaving Cambridge in the body, ate from the wrong tree at the same moment, so left it in the spirit also. In brief, he fell in love with and became engaged to Agnes Pembroke, a young woman not serious and not truthful and not saved; a bright, handsome, practical, efficient, cunning, ambitious, self-confident, hard, narrow, bustling, intellectually limited and inert young woman, bent on moulding him to her ambitions and desires. Rickie's love, which was merely a brief trick of nature's to entrap him, did not last long; when he came to he was securely in the trap and knew it. Knew it sooner and more clearly than is perhaps probable; here again Mr. Forster, writing from outside, paints from imagination shadows blacker and more clear-cut than would be painted by some one who had been inside the trap; the effect is of a clear, visible and conscious doom, perceived by Rickie himself and by all the perceptive people about him. Abandon hope, all ye who enter here, is written large upon his nuptials. The conflict of darkness with light is at its starkest.

While this dæmonic battle is waged, for our enthralment, on one plane, on the other, for our entertainment, Agnes, expression of the forces of imprisoning night, bustles briskly about, brightly solid and real. All she says is authentic: her conversations with Rickie are admirably and neatly true. I have earlier quoted one of them; here is another, also on literature. The two are in a restaurant; they are talking about Rickie's stories:

"'Can't you try something longer, Rickie?' she said. 'I believe we're on the wrong track. Try an out-and-out love-story.'

"'My notion just now,' he replied, 'is to leave the passions on the fringe.' She nodded, and tapped for the waiter . . . 'I can't soar; I can only indicate. That's where the musicians have the pull, for music has wings, and when she says "Tristan" and he says "Isolde," you are on the heights at once. What do people mean when they call love music artificial?'

"'I know what they mean, though I can't exactly explain.

Or couldn't you make your stories more obvious ? I don't see any harm in that. Uncle Willie floundered hopelessly. He doesn't read much, and he got muddled. I had to explain, and then he was delighted. Of course, to write down to the public would be another thing, and horrible. You have certain ideas, and you must express them. But couldn't you express them more clearly ? '

" ' You see—— ' He got no further than ' You see.'

" ' The soul and the body. The soul's what matters,' said Agnes, and tapped for the waiter again. He looked at her admiringly, but felt that she was not a perfect critic. Perhaps she was too perfect to be a critic. Actual life might seem to her so real that she could not detect the union of shadow and adamant that men call poetry. He would even go further and acknowledge that she was not as clever as himself—and he was stupid enough ! She did not like discussing anything or reading solid books, and she was a little angry with such women as did. It pleased him to make these concessions, for they touched nothing in her that he valued."

Rickie's Cambridge friends would, on this dialogue alone, have put Agnes firmly among the goats, in which flock he himself, though less firmly, being more given to tolerance, placed her brother Herbert, the schoolmaster. What was amiss with Herbert, he speculated ?

" The man was kind and unselfish ; more than that, he was truly charitable. . . . He was, moreover, diligent and conscientious : his heart was in his work . . . he was capable of affection : he was usually courteous and tolerant. Then what was amiss ? Why, in spite of all these qualities, should Rickie feel that there was something wrong with him—nay, that he was wrong as a whole, and that if the Spirit of Humanity should ever hold a judgment, he would assuredly be classed

among the goats ? The answer at first sight appeared a graceless one—it was that Herbert was stupid. Not stupid in the
ordinary sense—he had a business-like brain, and acquired
knowledge easily—but stupid in the important sense : his
whole life was coloured by a contempt of the intellect. That
he had a tolerable intellect of his own was not the point : it
is in what we value, not in what we have, that the test of us
resides . . . for all his fine talk about a spiritual life, he had
but one test for things—success : success for the body in this
life or for the soul in the life to come. And for this reason
Humanity, and perhaps such other tribunals as there may be,
would assuredly reject him."

Still more assuredly, by this test, would the
tribunals reject Agnes : and whether Rickie,
highly civilized and perceptive, would ever have
been conducted by love and imagination through
the stage of not remarking, or not minding, their
verdict on her, is questionable.

This, however, is after all only the usual problem which confronts us, both in literature and in
life, when persons of parts and sensibility are
observed to ally themselves with partners of mean
understanding, little information, and uncertain
tempers. And Agnes was presentable, handsome,
lively, kind, and glorified in Rickie's eyes by her
love for her dead lover ; she seemed to him a
Meredith heroine ; she encouraged him in his
writing ; she complained of dullness and propriety, told him she loved weirdness ; she enticed
and seduced and sirened him to her ; he, un-
critical and generous, exalted and rather silly, fell

at her feet. We have been prepared for it, for he
was told long since by candid friends that he was
in a dangerous state, that he liked people too
indiscriminately. Even footballers and rowing
men and the beefy set he liked, and Agnes came to
him a fine young woman, looking like a goddess,
clad in flowing green muslin like a mountain
cataract, nimbused with the tragic glory of her
dead love. She bade him be mean, and he thought
her wise ; she was insincere, mercenary, worldly,
and he thought her admirable, and it is all made to
seem a natural doom. Indeed, the only thing I
cannot accept in the affair is the birth of a child to
this couple ; what in the world, one is moved to
speculate, can have produced such a result ?

Agnes, as a portrait, is admirable; she is
one of the best-drawn young women in any novel.
Once or twice only the artist's sense of drama over-
draws her, carries her over the verge of normality
into what seems excess. There are startling hints
thrown out of moral obliquity in the young
woman. She is, it seems, cruel; she likes to think
of a small weak boy having been bullied at school
by her strong lover, she likes to hear of an unattractive boy having his ears brutally pulled by
his schoolfellows. With it, she is gloriously and
sensuously transformed by love, left permanently
a little queer by death. Her passions and emotions
are strong, her mind commonplace, her aims venal,
her methods dishonest. She is at once worse and

better than her foolish, harmless, tiresome brother, whom the tribunals would reject; she is a more subtle and a more sinister creation.

Rickie himself, the delicate, civilized, amiable, unlucky, perceptive creature, is one of those whom readers identify naturally with themselves (it is always the weak and sensitive characters in fiction who are thus identified, since practically every reader knows himself to be sensitive and weak)— making his problems and troubles their own. His marriage one takes as a horrid warning, the coils of Agnes seem to throttle one's own freedom. Rickie is the protagonist of a drama frighteningly near home. Yet there are things that I find unreal about Rickie, or perhaps merely odd. He is, for example, too tragically horrified by his belief that his dead father, whom he had always hated, had an illegitimate son. He faints, he is hysterical, he lives for years under a black shadow of disgust and fear. He adopts Agnes's view that his half-brother is " illicit, abnormal, worse than a man diseased . . . the fruit of sin, therefore sinful." He " became a sexual snob," like Agnes, who would almost have echoed the disgusted propriety of Mr. Allworthy's maid-servant, " it goes against me to touch these misbegotten wretches, whom I don't look upon as my fellow creatures. Faugh, how it stinks! It doth not smell like a Christian. If I might be so bold to give my advice, I would have it put in a basket and sent out. . . ." Agnes would no doubt have wished that her bastard half-brother-in-law might be put in a basket and sent out, but I doubt if Rickie's dislike for his father or love for his mother or his natural prudery would have produced, in one brought up to the habits of the Greek gods, so strong a reaction to a not, after all, surprising or very shocking fact. His maidish disgust seems to me to be one of the two distortions in the book.

The other, I think, is the character of Gerald Dawes, the lover of Agnes, who moves among the living figures lifeless; one cannot see or hear him. He is not really the kind of man Mr. Forster knows. Even his social background seems dubious: he is an officer, but cannot be quite a gentleman, though Agnes never observes it, for he talks of " undergrads," and of " being called a Varsity man and hobnobbing with lords." When Rickie shyly offers him some money to help him to get married, his anger is unaccountably excessive; and Rickie's decision not to marry for fear his children should inherit his lameness he condemns as " unhealthy " and unfit for the ears of " a lady."

He died that afternoon, broken up in a football match, and, though very sudden, it is not too soon, for Gerald has not come off. With the brainless athlete Mr. Forster is usually good, for he enjoys and likes him, whether he is modern English or ancient Athenian. But he does not like Gerald Dawes, and does not put him across. Against the hard opaqueness of this peevish-tempered bully, his pencil stubs its point and breaks; all we in the end get of Mr. Dawes is Agnes's love for him and the " flash of horror " with which Rickie remembers his contacts with him at school.

Among the intellectuals, the brilliant and stuck-up Ansell and his friends, Mr. Forster is, of course, so easily at home that he only has to present them, he need be at no pains. Ansell, whether or not he would have erupted and spouted with such scenic magnificence at a school lunch (and really I do not know why he should not, except that someone would have extinguished him before he threw up his flames so high) is alive throughout, as undergraduate philosopher, as damning and bitter-tongued friend, and as denunciatory angel. It is much more remarkable that his uneducated and philistine sister Maud should, in her brief appearances, be in her way as good. She is not by a single stroke touched up, pampered or romanticized as her brother a little is. She merely enters the Army and Navy Stores, has tea with Rickie and Agnes, makes some preposterous remarks about her brother and his missed fellowship, about philosophy, about the second spare room at home, and flounces out, spitefully baited by Agnes because she is not a lady. " Maud is a snob and a philistine," Rickie says, " but in her case something emerges." What emerges is that Maud is fundamentally decent, honest and first-hand; the tribunals will accept her, and so do we, though she does not, like Ansell and the " cynical ploughboy " Stephen, pretend to distinction or charm.

Stephen, the embodiment of his creator's appreciation of the instinctive, earthy life, is the magnificent foil to the ineffective civilization of Rickie, the violent intellectual austerity of Ansell, the cruel worldliness of Mrs. Failing, the conventional humbug of Agnes. He blooms, under Mr. Forster's hand, into a glorious pagan, a kind of visiting Phœbus of the Wiltshire downs, the most lovable of the unfettered creatures of earth whom the civilized delight to pet. Rickie, quoting to Mr. Pembroke the description of the Aristophanic young Athenian " perfect in body, placid in mind," who runs all day in the woods and meadows—" perhaps the most glorious invitation to the brainless life that has ever been given "— might have had Stephen in mind, though he was thus inaptly trying to describe Gerald Dawes. Mr. Forster does pet Stephen a little: true, he makes him faulty, crude, often intoxicated, we are told that he was coarse in habit and speech, he is irresponsible, and breaks anyhow one important promise, he is " somewhat a bully by nature." But he has a fine pride, he will not touch the money given him by his benefactress when she turns him out, he is beyond measure disgusted by the paltry meanness of Agnes. " Stephen,"

says Ansell, " is a bully; he drinks; he knocks
one down; but he would sooner die than take
money from people he did not love." Stephen is
the book's real hero. His likeableness is immense; he is perhaps the most likeable creature in
Mr. Forster's gallery. He lies naked on the roof
in the sun, drying after a bath, and tries to read
a manuscript story of Rickie's about a girl turning
into a tree.

> " The sloping gable was warm, and he lay back on it with
> closed eyes, gasping for pleasure. . . . ' Good ! Good ! ' he
> whispered. ' Good, oh good ! ' and opened the manuscript
> reluctantly.
> " What a production ! Who was this girl ? Where did she
> go to ? Why so much talk about trees ? ' I take it he wrote it
> when feeling bad,' he murmured, and let it fall into the gutter.
> It fell face downwards, and on the back he saw a neat little
> *résumé* in Miss Pembroke's handwriting, intended for such as
> him. ' Allegory. Man=modern civilization (in bad sense).
> Girl=getting into touch with Nature.'
> " In touch with Nature ! The girl was a tree ! He lit his
> pipe and gazed at the radiant earth. . . .
> " In touch with Nature ! What cant would the books think
> of next ? His eyes closed. He was sleepy. Good, oh good !
> Sighing into his pipe, he fell asleep."

This passage, as an indication of the characters
of Stephen, Rickie and Agnes, could scarcely be
bettered. There they all are, the pathetic imaginative writer, seeking life under worn-out
symbols, the shallow conventionalist, understanding neither symbols nor life, the lusty philistine,

scorning symbols and getting life at first hand.
Of the three, Mr. Forster and we sympathise with
and pity the first, dislike the second, and love the
third, with his enormous charm. In these reactions
we are with all the nice people, all the sheep, in
the book. The border case, the enigmatical sheep-
goat, who is fully aware of Stephen but is unkind
to him, becomes bored and throws him out, is
Mrs. Failing. Sister of Rickie's atrocious father,
with the Elliot faults and the Elliot cleverness,
selfish, bored, touchy, a malicious mischief-maker,
hard as nails, she seems to move between two
worlds. Drawn rather to a masculine pattern, she
suggests the selfish and testy elderly gentleman,
and gains therefrom a characteristic, slightly
epicene flavour, confounding the boundaries of
sex. Her interviews with Stephen are brilliant
comedy; those with Rickie and Agnes convince
less. We do not feel in her presence quite the
confidence of reality that Agnes gives us. What is
she up to ? How deep do her malice and her
mischief go ? She is possibly the most interesting
study in the book and, though we are not sure that
Mr. Forster feels sure of her, why should he ?
One does not feel sure of people in life, and there
is really no reason for all this Euclidean knowledge
of what they are and what they will do that novels
encourage in us. If Mrs. Failing remains a trifle
enigmatic, it is only as an elderly lady with whom
we are slightly acquainted should.

*The Longest Journey* showed its writer to be a character-creator of genius. Its people, whatever one may think of them, are alive, wittily actual, most intelligently themselves. They achieve significance in the intercourse and clash of contrasted ideas, that is to say, in the author's theme (for it must not be forgotten that this is his constant theme), without ever lapsing into humours or types: the theme emerges through them, it does not mould or twist them or pull their strings. If one should ask, is Mr. Forster more concerned with theme or people, the answer is that the two are to him one thing.

As to story, rhythm, technique, these are not, one feels, his principal business, yet they are all well shaped. The story falls naturally into its divisions—Cambridge, Sawston, Wiltshire—Truth and Life, Lies and Darkness, Recovery into Truth and Life (of another sort). Cambridge and Wiltshire are both idealized; Sawston blackened with Rickie's despair. The school, admirably presented, cannot have been so like an infernal circle as it seemed to Rickie; Cambridge not quite so like the blest kingdoms of joy and love where entertain him all the saints above in sweet societies; Wiltshire—but little is shirked in Wiltshire. Stephen breaks his promise and gets drunk; the lump of Wiltshire chalk slips from Rickie's fingers and breaks his delicate china cup (one of the admirable symbolic touches which Mr.

Forster uses unobtrusively and never overdoes);
the earth fails to confirm Rickie's confidence in
her: he dies whispering " You have been right "
to his aunt, who has warned him against this
confidence. In a brilliantly contrived and laconic
scene, Rickie finds Stephen at the village pub,
perjured and drunk. To kill Rickie immediately
afterwards in an act of heroic rescue presented a
temptation which was not resisted: let the novelist
who has not thus been tempted and fallen cast the
first stone, if he so desires; but let him not say
that the tragedy is not well and starkly reported,
or that the remaining and final chapter is not a
moving epilogue.

There are, of course, signs of adolescence in
the book. Cambridge, being too near, is too
golden a Utopia, too alma a mater; accidents
occur too suddenly, prove too fatal; the book
of essays by the deceased Mr. Failing is not,
one feels, a book that Mrs. Failing, Ansell, or
Mr. Forster would really admire, however the
critical world might have praised it (and, as we
know, the critical world, so incalculable and
capricious, has always been liable to praise practically anything). The extracts given from Mr.
Failing's essays are definitely platitudinous, wordy
and soft; literary parallels to him in all ages swim
in shoals to the mind. The mistake was probably
to quote from them.

Then there are moments when the mysticism

spouts and splashes a trifle, or expresses itself in dicta such as, " Ah, if he had seized those high opportunities! For they led to the highest of all, the symbolic moment, which, if a man accepts, he has accepted life." Definitely a splash, and one which the writer would not have made a little later. But such splashes are local and occasional, they do not weaken or blur the rhythm that carries the book through plot and time to its tragic climax and the tranquil close that is like a summer evening after rain.

The style is already far more developed than in the first novel: it stands pretty well up to the most trying demands made on it, pliable, sensitive, unobtrusively fraught with meaning, intelligence and passion. Less witty than it later became, it constantly holds the fleeting edge of a never-too-apparent smile. Here is the house of Mr. Pembroke, at Sawston school, where Rickie was to live:

" On the left of the entrance a large saffron drawing-room, full of cosy corners and dumpy chairs : here the parents would be received. On the right of the entrance a study, which he shared with Herbert : here the boys would be caned—he hoped not often. In the hall a framed certificate praising the drains, the bust of Hermes, and a carved teak monkey holding out a salver."

Here is Maud Ansell on her brother's missed fellowship:

" ' Mr. Elliot, you might know. Tell me. What is wrong with Stewart's philosophy ? What ought he to put in, or to alter, so as to succeed ? '

" Agnes, who knew better than this, smiled.

" ' I don't know,' said Rickie sadly. They were none of them so clever, after all.

" ' Hegel,' she continued vindictively. ' They say he's read too much Hegel. But they never tell him what to read instead. Their own stuffy books, I suppose. Look here—no, that's the *Windsor*.' After a little groping she produced a copy of *Mind*, and handed it round as if it was a geological specimen. ' Inside that there's a paragraph written about something Stewart's written about before, and there it says he's read too much Hegel, and it seems now that that's been the trouble all along.' Her voice trembled. ' I call it most unfair, and the fellowship's gone to a man who has counted the petals on an anemone.' "

Stephen Wonham is unconsciously funny every time he utters, and Herbert and Agnes Pembroke most times; the colloquy between Stephen and Herbert at the end, when Herbert, " now a clergyman," tries to cheat Stephen out of his profits on Rickie's stories, is superb. The humour throughout is a mixture of ironic slant and comment, and of the more extroverted wit that reveals itself in the uncommented conversations of the characters. On the whole, the irony wears oftener a sombre dress than in either of the novels which followed; it smiles more wryly, takes life more to heart. The most personally felt of the novels, it cuts nearest to the quick.

It was approved by the critics, though one of

them complained (perhaps rightly) that Gerald, " a British officer," would not have behaved as he did.

" Shall scarcely write another *Longest Journey*," the author wrote at the time. " It puzzled people so." It would seem that opinions on it were more divided than about any of the other books.

E

# CHAPTER V

## MODERN LITERATURE AND DANTE

THERE is printed in *The Working Men's College Journal* for January and February, 1907, a paper read by Mr. Forster to the Old Students' Club. It was named "Pessimism in Literature," and is worth noting, for at least two reasons: it expounds the artistic case for dwelling on sadness, on catastrophe, on death, as against the ordinary liver's choice of joy, of the happy and good circumstance and aspects of life; and it seeks to interpret the spirit of the age, as contrasted with that of other ages. The gist of his case for literary tragedy is, that art must seek what is permanent, even if it is sad, while "in life we seek what is gracious and noble, even if it is transitory." A little far-fetched, and one sees a more obvious case than this for assaulting the emotions of readers and audiences with griefs, for putting them "in a fiction, in a dream of passion"; tragic disasters are (to borrow Aristotle's word) the strongest psychogogues; they are, as the stage-struck young Milton wrote to Charles Diodati, "a pain to look at, and yet it is a pleasure to have looked and been pained, for sometimes there is a sweet bitterness in tears. The unhappy youth leaves his untasted joys and falls, a pitiful object, from his broken love. . . . Or the house of Pelops or noble Ilium is in grief, or the palace of Creon expiates its incestuous ancestry." The relish with which these unfortunate occurrences in the lives of others have invariably been applauded when enacted before us or narrated in literature is enough stimulus to the artist; he needs no other, he knows that misfortune and anguish are the very stuff of art, and the very stuff to give the reader and the groundlings. There is not, however, time to go into everything in a paper read to a club, and Mr. Forster had to get on to the spirit of the age, which was one of pessimism.

" For though the facts of human nature are constant, the spirit of humanity is not, but alters age by age, perhaps year by year, and like some restless child, continually groups the facts anew. Now it pushes the sad facts to the front, now the sorrowful ; to-day it has pushed to the front the fact that all things perish, the fact of evolution. . . . The artist of to-day, if he finds nothing cheerful, can at all events find consolation in sincerity. His pessimism results, not from wrong-headedness, not from blindness, but from an honest attempt to interpret the spirit of the age. Whether it is worth interpreting—that is a question too enormous. But he has to choose between sad art and no art. . . . We are so keenly—if you like, so morbidly—alive to sorrow and suffering, that human action seems impossible without them, and laughter impossible unless there is someone to laugh *at*—someone whom the laughter would pain if he knew of it. . . . Even in life, practical jokes are rather shocking. The world grows so frightfully cultured and kind that old gentlemen who slip upon orange peel are no longer what they were."

To-day, in a world reverted to normal, grown once more, if it had ever ceased to be so, frightfully uncultured and most frightfully unkind, the old gentleman on his orange peel would appear to have come again into his kingdom. But has he ever left it ? One feels sure that even in the sensitive Edwardian age he would have got his laugh all right from the majority in all lands. Mr. Forster, in making his comments, was speaking for the cultured, kind and compassionate minority, he had fallen into the snare that has always trapped the intellectual. Real unkind fun, he thought, was no longer the joy it had been, and compares poor tormented Malvolio as Shakespeare wrote him, a figure of riotous fun, a cockshy, with Malvolio as piteously acted by our modern actors, Benson and Tree, and with Shaw's attitude towards the Irishmen who laugh at the sufferings of the pig hurt in a car accident. " Here," he says, " the modern mind has progressed: if it is a progress. It has detected the discomfort and misery that lie so frequently beneath the smiling surface of things. But what it has gained in insight it has lost in power. It can be witty and sarcastic and amusing. But it can never recall joy on a large scale—the joy of the gods."

This is one of the things that sensitive minds

have always felt about the age they lived in; we feel it to-day, and one hears it attributed, by those whose memories do not reach back across that gulf, to the tragedy of the European war and the uneasy years of fear which have followed it. But here is Mr. Forster saying the same thing thirty years ago, and with equal truth. And thirty years before that, George Eliot and Samuel Butler and other sensitive persons were saying it, and before these Charles Reade and Tennyson and the Brontës, and Shelley and Coleridge, Horace Walpole, Swift, Steele, Dryden, and Montaigne; and Donne and other poets often wrote as if they took it too much for granted to trouble to mention it. And they may all have been quite right, and, if so, in what abyss of desolation shall we end ? But, however right the view of our increasing sensitiveness may be, it is obviously a delusion to attribute much sensitiveness to the world at large in any age, the world being mostly cheerful toughs who will laugh at the tortured pig and crowd round a prison where a man is being hanged. The " modern mind " must include the minds of the music-hall public, of a Bank Holiday crowd, and of writers such as Mr. P. G. Wodehouse, who do deal in solid, unadulterated single-minded mirth.

Still, one sees what Mr. Forster meant, and so did his audience, who, carrying on the discussion thus opened, went much farther, and remarked that pessimism was general, and much to be deplored; one gentleman had spent his holidays at Berne, " which we might think would be a cheerful place, surrounded as it was with beautiful mountain scenery, and with no foreign affairs to trouble its people, but no, even Berne was affected with the prevailing joylessness, and many young Swiss were so imbued with the despondency of the age that, rather than live, they chose to end their lives by throwing themselves from the precipices with which their country abounded." Music was in the same plight; the speaker had heard a piece by Richard Strauss in Berlin and Vienna, where it was received with hisses in which he joined cordially. Pessimism did not seem to him the right way in which to face the drudgery of life. It was deplorable, and all these pessimistic writers such as Zola, Ibsen and Shaw left a bad taste in the mouth. This was the majority feeling of the meeting, one speaker observing that if there was really a widespread demand for pessimistic literature, this was to be deplored as a symptom of racial senility, another that the world was quite sufficiently full of trouble, and that pessimistic books were a rascally injustice to readers. It was a good discussion, and must have been a useful and agreeable contribution to Mr. Forster's knowledge of the modern mind.

If we have lingered too long over it, let us hasten on to his lectures that Lent on Dante, " whom,"

he has a preliminary note, " I cannot like," but
whom he possibly came to like as he prepared the
lectures; or possibly not very much. The notes
for these lectures, attractively colloquial, speculative, first-hand and free from text-bookery, show,
as one would expect, sympathy with Dante, and
with many of the unfortunate souls, and some
irritated distaste for officials, such as the austere
cicerone and the venerable warder Cato. " Is V.'s
behaviour supposed by D. to be that of the ideal
pedagogue ?  I fear so," is the note on Virgil's
rather nagging rebuke of the poet for stumbling
sleepily along, wrapped in contemplation. As
to Cato, he is disliked from the first Canto of the
*Purgatorio*. " The chilliness of Heaven appears
already . . . he admits the poets only because a
' *donna del ciel* ' has sent them. His manner very
official." Later, while Casella is pausing on the
way to Paradise to sing a love song to Dante and
the saved souls, Cato bustles up and " sends the
redeemed souls about their business," breaking up
the singing with " *Che è ciò, spiriti lenti? Qual
negligenza. . . . Correte. . . .*" and Mr. Forster's
sympathies are all with the dilatory and singing
souls. " The spirit of the Renaissance is in this
episode. But Dante, though sympathetic to
human yearnings, records their negation with
cheerfulness. He *could* see the pathos of this dis-
turbed concert, but, with a happy dignity, refuses
to do so.  Casella, who forgets the ' *nuova legge*, '

and Cato, who embodies it, are both recorded
benignly. (I don't like the type, though!) "

Whether the type he does not like is the
benignly impartial Dante or the legalistic Cato,
he is, anyhow, for the Renaissance against
Medievalism every time. Virgil's exposition of
the fruitless attempts of human reason to travel
the way of infinity, which is held by the Trinity,
and of the eternal grief of the pre-Christian philosophers over their chronological solecism, is
annotated, " Medieval self-complacency." And,
when Virgil rebukes Dante for thinking of two
things at once, " Contrast the Renaissance pliancy.
Medievalism makes for stiffness—not, I think,
for strength." Of the paved way whereon Dante
saw so clearly all the proud fallen creatures of the
past, " No sense of mystery or history. Why
should there be ? The world had always been open
to God. Creation v. evolution. The latter gives
more scope to the imagination."

What rouses his enthusiasm is the poetry, the
splendour and beauty of imagery, and characterization when it appears. He has constant applause
for these. " They cleanse themselves in the Dawn.
The staging magnificent. Cato has disappeared
like a tiresome prologue, and the curtain rises
upon the trembling seas and dewy meadows."
" We pass from scholasticism to poetry. Re-
capture of the mountain atmosphere, too often
lost," and so on. Throughout, too, the novelist

is looking for character, personality. Sordello's entrance he hails as " the first personality after Manfred; though Dante, unlike Virgil, is never content with an epithet, and tries to vivify even minor characters by some historical touch." He wishes that " D. would discuss V. more often." Of Dante's own character and personality as they show themselves he takes constant notice, remarking his venomous human outbursts against this and that bugbear in Italy, his often tasteless classical allusions, which he explains by " D. misses the point of the Antique, but feels a certain poetry in it which he expects to transfigure a slovenly allusion." Dante emerges as an eager, enquiring, analytical, blundering poet, a little intimidated by the majestic authority of his master, a little breathless and confused at the place in which he finds himself, torn this way and that by sympathy, pity, admiration, speculation and wonder, subject, like all poets, to collapses of invention and imagination, recalled from poetry too often by scholastic discussion; a poet with one foot in the Renaissance, the other in Medievalism, engaged, as a note on the *Vita Nuova* puts it, in " discussions sometimes merely scholastic, sometimes eternally true, sometimes fantastic. Mixture of learning and self-analysis makes it difficult to read him in these matters."

¶ How ungenial D. is! " is a note on *De Monarchia*. " Impossible to love him, or to feel

that he said a kind word to a chap in passing.
Even when passion is good, it must come last."
But this estimate is modified in the *Purgatorio*
notes.

For the rest, these lectures, adequate historically
and critically, must have been both entertaining
and imaginatively stimulating. Dante and E. M.
Forster are in odd but happy juxtaposition. The
gigantic medieval poet and scholar, steeped in
the theological beliefs of Christendom, using his
dreams, mysticism, passions, inventions, tremendous reading, and soaring literary and poetic
power within the bounds of the theology and
geosophy of his epoch, yet creating a world of
living, tragic human creatures, is approached and
examined by a product of modern liberal and
rational humanism, a classic, an æsthete, an
agnostic, a novelist, a wit, a man whose culture is
of Cambridge, not of Florence, yet many of whose
beliefs about life, and much of whose religion, are
fundamentally the same. For both are mystics;
both believe in the eternal meanings of human
choices, the eternal value of men's relationships
with their fellows, and with something that, quite
differently envisaged, may for brevity's sake be
called God. Both believe passionately in salvation
and in damnation; the *Commedia* is not fuller of
lost souls and saved souls and souls struggling
in Purgatory than are Mr. Forster's *commedie*.
Again and again one sees parallels. Both know

that there is a Way, which can be lost in a dark wood, and found again. The first Canto of the *Inferno* might be a description of Rickie Elliot's inner life in the dark wood of Sawston and marriage, when " *la diritta via era smarrita,*" and " *tanto è amara, che poco è più morte* "; or of Lucy Honeychurch's refusal to face truth. Both believe in following the sun of truth and reality, " *che mena diritto altrui per ogni calle,*" which leads men straight on every road, which led Rickie from his wife, Lucy to her lover, conducted Stephen Wonham through his direct, unthinking, instinctive life, Ansell through his unprofitable scholar's researches, Margaret Schlegel through her eager experiments and contacts, Adela Quested to her confession of truth in the witness-box. Both believe that men can, by their own choice, enter the regions of darkness for ever, and join " *le genti dolorose ch'hanno perduto il ben dell' intelletto,*" and that one way of doing so is to sin against life, to make the great refusal—" this is the miserable state of those sad souls who lived without infamy and without praise; they are mixed with the bad choir of those angels who were neither rebellious nor faithful to God. . . . Heaven drove them out, to save its beauty from diminishment, and neither will the deep hell receive them. . . . Their blind life is so mean that they are envious of every other lot . . . they never were alive." It might be said of them, as of the souls that perished through avarice, that their undiscerning life had made them too obscure for recognition.

Dante and Mr. Forster would, one may assume, dislike one another's theologies, politics and attitudes towards life. Had they encountered one another in hell or purgatory, they would have been distant, and the Master would have discouraged his pupil from any attitude but shocked disapproval; had Mr. Forster been among the souls, we may be sure that a terrific punishment would have been devised for him by the poet who with such stern relish thought up unspeakable (but not at all so by him) manglings and tortures and filth for heretics. Mr. Forster, in his turn, would have been revolted by Dante's ingenuity in these departments of invention, by his sternness to the great pre-Christians, his harshness to the fleshly sins, and, as he puts it, his ungeniality, and (a little) by his toadying meekness to the pedagogic Virgil. Had they discussed politics, they must have fallen out, for, in addition to his acid and vindictive bitterness on the intricacies of local Italian feuds, that his Master ought surely to have bidden him forget and put behind him, and into which Mr. Forster would have found it difficult to enter fully, Dante had his firm faith in a divine monarchy, in the Roman Emperor as God-controlled totalitarian dictator of the earth, and here sympathies would have been too imperfect, and based on premises too widely apart, and experiences too alien, to make a good discussion. What, then, would they have shared ? Interest in people, in history, and in human character; admiration for grandeur, in scenery, humanity, and literature; a tendency to discuss points which Virgil found irrelevant, and to dawdle a little on the way; and, beneath their so different views on cosmology and theology, a mystic belief in the greatness of life and in the strange powers that haunt us, in salvation, damnation, struggle, eternal victory and eternal loss. So that the encounter, though somewhat questionable and risky, might have worked out, if it had chanced to take the right turn, not too badly after all.

# CHAPTER VI

## A ROOM WITH A VIEW

DURING this year, 1907, Mr. Forster was engaged also on short stories (one was *The Celestial Omnibus*) and on the new version and the completion of *A Room with a View*, of which he had written a draft of the first half in 1903. Of this, " My story distracts me," he writes. " Clear and bright and well constructed, but so thin." It is true that it is clearer and brighter, and possibly better constructed, than *The Longest Journey*, and thinner in the sense of being less full and rich. But it has a wit, a gay brilliance, that belongs, perhaps, to Mr. Forster's notion of Italy. *The Longest Journey* is partly mist-bound, and mostly unhappy. *A Room with a View*, though more than half of it occurs in Surrey, is dominated by the first, the Italian section; the English drama is played against this background, before an audience who know that *Italiam petimus*, and that, until we return there we shall be living in a foolish mental fog, in, as the spokesman for Italy, love and truth, old Mr. Emerson (who is not really so bad as this sounds, though he does admire Ruskin) puts it to the groping and erring Lucy, a muddle. Rickie

Elliot lived and died in a muddle; he got as far
as Wiltshire, but never as far as Italy. But Lucy
Honeychurch, charming, ingenuous, uncultured
and naïve, arrives in a Florentine *pension* with her
revolting middle-aged cousin Charlotte (the only
unpleasant elderly lady in Mr. Forster's gallery
of these) on her first visit to Italy, aged twenty-
two.

The comedy opens with zest. The ladies,
betrayed by the landlady, have been given poor
rooms, which do not look out on the Arno, they
look north, they look on courtyards, they smell;
the ladies are sadly vexed. At dinner, kind and
uncouth old Mr. Emerson, a fellow guest, who
has no delicacy but does beautiful things in a tact-
less way, intrudes into their discontented dialogue
with " I have a view, I have a view." Miss Bartlett is startled. She perceives the intruder to be
ill-bred, and one cannot be too careful, particularly
with a young girl in charge. He proceeds to em-
barrass her with the suggestion that the ladies
should change rooms with him and his son George,
who also has a view (and I have always felt that,
had I been his son George, I could not have forgiven him). Miss Bartlett, offended, says that this
is quite out of the question. The other guests,
being the better class of tourist, sympathize
with the newcomers; they have already decided
that the Emersons do not do. There ensues an
argument, during which " Lucy had an odd feeling

that whenever these ill-bred tourists spoke the contest widened and deepened till it dealt, not with rooms and views, but with—well, with something quite different, whose existence she had not realized before."

Thus, then, the scene is laid; all set for the struggle between good and evil powers that, for all Mr. Forster's wit, his exquisite character-drawing, his deft expression of shades of feeling, of quirks of personality, of all the lively play of the human scene, is as much the real matter of his dramas as it is that of a medieval morality play. Good and evil dæmons fight, in that *pension* dining-room and throughout the book, for possession of the ingenuous heart and soul of Lucy. On one side of the battle are ranged the Emersons, truth, freedom, nature, love, music (Lucy plays the piano triumphantly, though inaccurately, and her mother complains that it upsets her), the Italian lower orders, and a view; on the other Charlotte, prim propriety, false feelings, the conventions, the English bourgeoisie, rooms without views, and a priggish young man Cecil Vyse. In this battle, which may be called for short Truth *v.* Sham, there are a number of skirmishes, but until just on the end it would seem that Sham, despite an occasional set-back caused by a burst of music, of love, or of a fine view, is winning hands down. It is easily the victor in the first, the Florentine section of the story; truth and love, routed and shamed, slink into the hidden recesses of Lucy's soul, to be overlaid with all the sly deceptions she can devise to keep them quiet while she plays her part in the conventional world of lies.

It is another form of the conflict of *The Longest Journey*. Lucy's simple, instinctive soul, Rickie Elliot's, tortured and civilized, are battle-grounds for the same kind of good and evil forces.

In very similar passages, the victory of the darkness is described.

> " It did not do to think, nor, for the matter of that, to feel. She gave up trying to understand herself, and joined the vast armies of the benighted, who follow neither the heart nor the brain, and march to their destiny by catch-words. The armies are full of pleasant and pious folk. But they have yielded to the only enemy that matters—the enemy within. They have sinned against passion and truth, and vain will be their strife after virtue. As the years pass, they are censured. Their pleasantry and their piety show cracks, their wit becomes cynicism, their unselfishness hypocrisy ; they feel and produce discomfort wherever they go. They have sinned against Eros and Pallas Athene, and not by any heavenly intervention, but by the ordinary course of nature, these allied deities will be avenged.

> " Lucy entered this army when she pretended to George that she did not love him, and pretended to Cecil that she loved no one. The night received her as it had received Miss Bartlett thirty years before."

And we know what it had made of poor Miss Bartlett. (This is, by the way, the only hint we get of what had made Miss Bartlett what she was, and it is tantalizing.)

F

One compares this with Rickie Elliot's plight,
when, after yielding to his wife and consenting to
continue deceiving Stephen about their relationship, he settled down to deteriorate, and " the
spiritual part of him proceeded towards ruin."
The account of Rickie is more moving, for it is
not didactic, not a sermon; its author was feeling
more adult when he wrote it.

In both books sham wins until near the end,
when truth prevails, not without dust and heat,
indeed with a violent upheaval and rending of life.
The difference here is that the star-crossed Rickie
dies in unrelieved despair, believing truth to have
failed him and broken in his hands, while Lucy
lives and is to be happy and free, the only serious
casualty in truth's final victorious engagement
with her being her mother's affection, but this, it is
obvious, will recover, since Mrs. Honeychurch
(Mr. Forster's most agreeable creation among
elderly ladies) is really on the angels' side, and can
herself have no patience with sham.

There is, of course, some over-assertion and
intrusion of the spiritual issues involved, and
some didacticism. Later, when more practised at
his job, Mr. Forster left general views on life to
be expressed more (never wholly) by the actors in
his dramas, and less explicitly than through reflec-
tion and action. *A Room with a View* was written
by a young writer (its conception and first draft by
a very young writer) in an epoch more didactic

as to spiritual principles, though less as to political, than this, and fiction had a fashion of Maeter-linckian moral generalizations which would be disconcerting to-day. Brilliant novelists now are seldom open moralists; the issues of fiction—perhaps a little of life?—have changed. " Here are some people: here is what I think they said and did and felt. I do not know what they meant by it, nor if they meant anything, nor where they are going, nor why. Take them or leave them; this is what they were and did." I do not think that any English or French novelist was saying just this in the early years of the century. Tchekov had for some years been saying it, but in Russian, and his influence was not widely felt in England until he could be read in English. Mr. Forster, an Edwardian, still expressed his views occasion-ally in the Maeterlinck mode.

It is, naturally, not the spiritual battles, not truth nor Eros nor Pallas Athene, that hold our interest through the book; I can even imagine being bored by these sublime beings and their wrestlings. I can imagine it: in point of fact, I never was; encountering the enchanting book at a susceptible age, I sucked up every word, hung enthralled, and cannot quite recover from this early attitude. But one knows that it does not do; that what is brilliant and remarkable in the book is not the high-flown G. F. Wattsian bits about truth and love and life, and not the story, but the superb cast, their conversations and relationships and mutual reactions. It was Mr. Forster's third novel, and he was pouring out his characters as lavishly and zestfully as if he had no future to save for. He might see Life as he liked; he might feel it to be a Beethoven symphony, " gusts of splendour, gods and demi-gods contending with vast sounds, colour and fragrance broadcast on the field of battle, magnificent victory, magnificent death ": his triumph is that he was able to put across this dramatic (and on one plane quite accurate) view through the medium of a most delicate and witty comedy of relationships and personalities assembled in a Florence *pension* and in a corner of Surrey. The outrageous lady novelist, the pair of gentle and garrulous little travelling spinsters, the good clergyman, the bad clergyman, the touching Emersons, the dreadful Charlotte Bartlett, the ingenuous Lucy, the Italian *vetturino*, the delightful Honeychurches, the egregious Cecil, even the Surrey country neighbours, tread the pattern of the dance sure-footed, at once firmly themselves and relevant parts of the whole. It is an extraordinarily likeable book; one would say amiable, were it not a word so often misused and profaned. Take, for example, the Honeychurches. Mrs. Honeychurch and her son Freddy are two of the most finished round portraits in Mr. Forster's gallery. All that either says is precisely right; they function in

their comfortable, commonplace Surrey home
with the solid positiveness and brightness of the
figures in a Guache painting; there is no false
touch. Take up Mrs. Honeychurch anywhere
you like; driving back from a garden party with
her daughter and her daughter's clever and stuck-
up young man; talking at a meal; writing a letter;
confronted on a walk in the woods with her son,
an unknown young man, and the vicar, all running
naked round a pond.

" ' Gracious alive ! ' cried Mrs. Honeychurch. ' Whoever
were those unfortunate people ? Oh, dears, look away ! And
poor Mr. Beebe too ! Whatever has happened ? '

" ' Come this way immediately,' commanded Cecil. . . .
He led them towards the bracken where Freddy sat concealed.

" ' Oh, poor Mr. Beebe ! Was that his waistcoat we left in
the path ? Cecil, Mr. Beebe's waistcoat——' . . . .

" ' Well, *I* can't help it,' said a voice close ahead, and Freddy
reared a freckled face and a pair of snowy shoulders out of the
fronds. ' I can't be trodden on, can I ? '

" ' Good gracious me, dear ; so it's you ! What miserable
management ! Why not have a comfortable bath at home, with
hot and cold laid on ? '

" ' Look here, mother : a fellow must wash, and a fellow's
got to dry, and if another fellow——'

" ' Dear, no doubt you're right as usual, but you are in no
position to argue. Come, Lucy.' They turned ' Oh, look—
don't look ! Oh, poor Mr. Beebe ! How unfortunate
again——'

" For Mr. Beebe was just crawling out of the pond. . . .

" ' Emerson, you beast, you've got on my bags.'

" ' Hush, dears,' said Mrs. Honeychurch, who found it
impossible to remain shocked. ' And do be sure you dry

yourselves thoroughly first. All these colds come of not drying thoroughly. . . .'

" ' Hullo ! ' cried George, so that again the ladies stopped. . . .

" ' Bow, Lucy ; better bow. Whoever is it ? I shall bow.' "

A simple social disaster of country life, in which each actor plays his characteristic part, and Mrs. Honeychurch, without the use of tact, delicacy, prudery, or anything but cheerful and amiable good sense, turns it into a gay and comic contre-temps. She has the eternal, breezy, unsubtle, maternal, philistine humour of her kind; she discusses the servants, the garden, domestic problems, the neighbours, and makes her æsthetic highbrow future son-in-law, Cecil, wince at every turn. She is anti-humbug, anti-culture, anti-pretentiousness, anti-pose, anti-sham; she is, in brief, on the angels' side every time, as Cecil, compact of humbug, culture, pretentiousness, pose and sham, is every time on the devil's. (Culture, it may in passing be noted, fights on different fronts in Mr. Forster's battles; in *A Room with a View*, *Where Angels Fear to Tread*, and some of the short stories, it is with the devils; in *Howards End* on the whole with the angels; in *The Longest Journey*, it and philistinism are to be found, eclectically, on both sides.)

A more enigmatic character, one of Mr. Forster's few enigmatic characters, is the pleasant clergyman, Mr. Beebe. He seems, through most of the book, all that a man and a brother should be, humorous, tolerant, broadminded, kindly, sympathetic. He dislikes humbug, Cecil, Charlotte, and all the wrong people; he enjoys the Emersons, the Honeychurches, and human nature. We count on him to support the right cause, to assist Lucy's escape from Cecil, Charlotte and humbug, to help her and George Emerson to freedom. And we are quite wrong, he does nothing of the sort. Delighted though he is when Lucy gets rid of Cecil, he is surprisingly and irrationally disgusted when she announces her affection for George; it is he who stiffens her mother against the marriage and keeps her unnaturally unforgiving after it. This is really not properly explained. Mr. Forster maintains that the clergyman's Pauline preference for celibacy was enough to account for it.

> " 'They that marry do well, but they that refrain do better.' So ran his belief, and he never heard that an engagement was broken off but with a slight feeling of pleasure. . . . The feeling was very subtle and quite undogmatic, and he never imparted it to any other of the characters in this entanglement. Yet it existed, and it alone explains his action subsequently, and his influence on the action of others."

Of course it does not explain it. Mr. Beebe remains obscure, only, I fear, to be explained by the fact that his creator does not care for clergymen. He liked Mr. Beebe, and made him a pleasant personality; but, at the point when it served the needs of the situation, he caused him to recede from his own character into a mystic irrationality suitable to his cloth, saying, as it were, " Well, the man's a parson, and I'm going to make him behave as such, or rather, as I choose that parsons shall behave." So exit nice, worldly-wise, cultured Mr. Beebe, and enter a stern medieval priest breathing thunder against defaulters from his strange code. I do not believe in this, and do not really believe in Mr. Forster's belief in it. Still, he might reply, people are so strange, life so odd, so full of unnaturalness, that practically anyone may do anything, and does. So let Mr. Beebe's odd turn pass. It removes him, anyhow, still further from any conventional category.

Old Mr. Emerson one is not sure about. Starting at the *pension* dinner-table as a charming, kind, blunt old man, proceeding, as he goes about Florence, to garrulous and disarming crudities, he shows himself soon a sentimental preacher about Life, and ends by persuading Lucy to free her soul and marry his son. A likeable old man, but his last speeches are too nobly eloquent to sound true. They may, however, be so: self-educated, socialist and rationalist old men *were* sometimes nobly eloquent about Life. Are there to-day fewer such old men, less magniloquence and less magnanimity ? If so, it is a pity, for Mr. Emerson, though he talks too much and is too much soaked in the publications of the Rationalist Press Association and perhaps in the more symbolic pictures of G. F. Watts, is charming. He believes in universal brotherhood, and probably the war would have turned him into a militant pacifist and broken his heart.

There is little doubt that it would have turned George into a conscientious objector. George, a grave and troubled young man, admirably laconic of speech and direct in method, has in him enough of his father (who carves mottoes on furniture) to pin up over his washstand a sheet of paper on which he has scrawled a large mark of interrogation. George is attractive, touching, and perfectly real; he makes an admirable foil to his garrulous father and to the cultured Cecil.

Four of his creatures Mr. Forster thoroughly dislikes—the Reverend Cuthbert Eager, the English chaplain at Florence; Miss Lavish, the novelist; Charlotte Bartlett; Cecil Vyse (in this order). By any standards, they are noxious: comparing them with the characters in his other books whom, in varying degrees, he dislikes, one can arrive at Mr. Forster's main test for human beings. One thinks of the dreadful Harriet Herriton; of Gerald Dawes and the Pembrokes; of Charles Wilcox; of Ronny Heaslop and his fellow Anglo-Indians; of the pompous Mr. Worters in *Other Kingdom*; of spiteful Mrs. Failing.

All these people are what are called gentlefolk;

most, though not all, are stupid, and lack perceptiveness; about half are, or might be, liars. But one thing they all have in common: they do not like people.

" ' He is the sort who are all right so long as they keep to things—books, pictures—but kill when they come to people,' says George Emerson of Cecil Vyse. . . . ' I saw him first in the National Gallery, when he winced because my father mispronounced the names of great painters. Then he brings us here, and we find it is to play some silly trick on a kind neighbour. That is the man all over—playing tricks on people, on the most sacred form of life that he can find.' "

" You're the sort," Lucy tells Cecil, " who can't know anyone intimately." Or, in Freddy's phrase, he was " the kind of fellow who would never wear another fellow's cap." " It would be wrong not to loathe that man," says Cecil of a harmless country gentleman. Lucy thinks,

" If Cecil disliked Sir Harry Otway and Mr. Beebe, what guarantee was there that the people who really mattered to her would escape ? For instance, Freddy. Freddy was neither clever, nor subtle, nor beautiful, and what prevented Cecil from saying, any minute, ' It would be wrong not to loathe Freddy ' ? "

Breaking off her engagement, Lucy accuses him,

" ' You don't like Freddy, nor my mother. . . . You despise my mother—I know you do—because she's conventional and bothers over puddings. . . . You wrap yourself up in art and music and would try to wrap up me. I won't be stifled, not by the most glorious music, for people are more glorious, and you hide them from me. That's why I break off my engagement. You were all right as long as you kept to things, but when you came to people——' "

Rather a narrow gulf seems to divide Cecil's misanthropy from that of Rickie Elliot's Cambridge friends, who complained that he was in a dangerous state, for he was trying to like people, and succeeding. The gulf is partly that of the years between undergraduates and an adult man who should have learnt better long since, and partly one of different standards of judgment. Ansell and his friends did, indeed, damn the beefy men of their college on the same grounds on which Cecil despised Freddy Honeychurch, but probably after leaving Cambridge they would have rather liked Freddy had they met him; Ansell did, in fact, like the definitely beefy Stephen Wonham immensely, though, in the unlikely circumstance of Stephen having been up at King's with him, he might not then have regarded him as among the saved. (Cecil would probably have been bored with him at any time, after a brief period of drawing him out for his own entertainment.) Ansell's test qualities for people were seriousness and truthfulness; Cecil's were culture and intellectual and social " rightness." Ansell would have liked the two Emersons, and would not have despised Mrs. Honeychurch for talking about food and servants, though he might have been bored. Cecil is an intellectual snob.

" ' Whenever I speak,' says Mrs. Honeychurch, ' he winces.
. . . No doubt I am neither artistic nor literary nor intellectual
nor musical, but I cannot help the drawing-room furniture :
your father bought it and we must put up with it, will Cecil
kindly remember.'

" ' I—I see what you mean, and certainly Cecil oughtn't.
But he does not mean to be uncivil . . . he is easily upset by
ugly things—he is not unkind to *people*.'

" ' Is it a thing or a person when Freddy sings ? '

" ' You can't expect a really musical person to enjoy comic
songs as we do.'

" ' Then why didn't he leave the room ? Why sit wriggling
and sneering and spoiling everyone's pleasure ? ' . . ."

The same misanthropy marks the hateful Mr.
Eager. How rude he is to the Florentine photo-
graph-seller, with his " Andate via! Andate
presto, presto! " How harsh and unkind to the
young *vetturino* and his girl! How vindictive and
malicious about Mr. Emerson! How he despises
the poor, hating them to ascend socially! In brief,
he dislikes people. He looks at them from inside
a hostile fence.

" Now," says Lucy to Cecil, " a clergyman that
I do hate, a clergyman that does have fences, and
the most dreadful ones, is Mr. Eager, the English
chaplain at Florence. . . . He was a snob, and so
conceited, and he did say such unkind things."

Miss Lavish, the novelist, only likes people for
the sake of using them in a book. She hates her
fellow-countrymen abroad.

" Oh, the Britisher abroad! . . . Look at their

figures! They walk through my Italy like a pair
of cows. It's very naughty of me, but I would like
to set an examination paper at Dover, and turn
back every tourist who couldn't pass it."

For Miss Bartlett there is more hope: she is
" not withered up all through," and perhaps her
failure to be saved depends more on a foolish
egoism and sense of injury than on disliking
people; still, " dreadful, frozen Charlotte! How
cruel she would be to a man like that! " (a cab-
driver soliciting custom).

As to Harriet Herriton, she hates practically
everyone, and lives in a chronic bad temper. So,
in a slightly modified and less embittered way,
do Charles Wilcox and Gerald Dawes, both of
whom go in for firm and hearty contempt.

The two Pembrokes like no one objectively,
only in relation to themselves and their own
advantage. To imagine either of them thinking,
how delightful so-and-so is, is out of the question.
They are not cantankerous; they are merely self-
centred, they could never be good fellows, any
more than the bored Mrs. Failing or the smug
Mr. Worters of *Other Kingdom* could be good
fellows.

Ronny Heaslop and his fellow countrymen in
India confine themselves to disliking the natives
of India and those who do not dislike these.
Ronny snubs and ignores the two educated
Indians with whom he finds Adela Quested

conversing. " He did not mean to be rude to the
two men, but the only link he could be conscious
of with an Indian was the official, and neither
happened to be his subordinate. As private individuals he forgot them." Like the other English,
he sneers continually at Indians in the mass, calling
them " the Aryan brother." Actually what they
feel is dislike. So utterly does this damn them
with Mr. Forster that they behave, as the book
goes on, fantastically ill: they have forfeited all
claim on his wide human sympathies, they have
committed the unforgivable sin, rejecting and
despising human beings, and from this damned
dislike of humanity, other failures of character,
intelligence and reality naturally spring. How
strangely some of these misanthropes behave!
Cecil Vyse, for example. He does not even know
how to be in love. He is a *précieux ridicule*:
changing the gender, he might echo Cathos with
her " *Comment est-ce qu'on peut souffrir la pensée de
coucher contre un homme vraiment nu ?* " In love,
he breathes an air not native to him. Several days
after his acceptance by Lucy, Mr. Forster asks us
to believe that he has not yet kissed her. Walking
with her in a wood, " a certain scheme, from which
hitherto he had shrunk, now appeared practical. . . .

    " ' Lucy, I want to ask something of you that I have never
asked before.'
    " At the serious note in his voice she stepped frankly and
kindly towards him.

" ' What, Cecil ? '

" ' Hitherto never—not even that day on the lawn when you agreed to marry me——'

" He became self-conscious and kept glancing round to see if they were observed. His courage had gone.

" ' Yes ? '

" ' Up to now I have never kissed you.'

" She was as scarlet as if he had put the thing most indelicately.

" ' No—more you have," she stammered.

" ' Then I ask you—may I now ? '

" ' Of course you may, Cecil. You might before. I can't run at you, you know.' "

The embrace that follows is naturally not a great success, and after it, embarrassed, they walk away in silence.

Of course this is preposterous. Mr. Forster has made Cecil something sub or super human. The only counterpart to him that I can at the moment remember is a young man called Norman May, in *The Daisy Chain*, by Charlotte Yonge, who proposes to a young lady whom he loves while on a walk with her, and is accepted, after which, much embarrassed, they walk home on opposite sides of the road, a scene which my mother, reading this admirable book aloud to us in my childhood, assured us out of her riper experience was improbable. We did not care. We had no desire that Norman, whom we admired, should demean himself and make himself soppy kissing a girl. Norman was meant for better things; he was, in fact, to be a missionary to the heathen. By all means let him keep on the far side of the road, and not let himself get what it was our habit to call " kissy."

Cecil, though he was not to be a missionary, suffered from the same inhibitions; he is dehumanized beyond reason. His distaste for the body, for all physical energies and functions, would not, one feels, have carried him so far. Mr. Forster, having put him on the wrong side of the fence, among the inhuman who war against youth and life and the run of the blood, gives the effect of fumbling with him, overdoing, presenting not a person but a conception.

This, however, is only so when he is too closely and intimately inspected, for he repels intimacy. Socially, when wincing at Mrs. Honeychurch and her friends, or coming the highbrow over Lucy, or snubbing Freddy, Cecil is all that could be desired, and plays his part well in the gay pattern of the whole.

Lucy, on the other hand, is good throughout, and is a remarkable example of a simple and perfectly real young woman drawn both objectively and subjectively by a sophisticated male writer. Would she have repulsed George for so long ? Probably not: one must allow some concessions to a plot. Would she have been so overwhelmed by a sudden kiss on a picnic expedition ? Were Edwardian young ladies so sensitive, their honour so quaint ? No; again, one must allow for the plot. Lucy was not silly, and her fuss about the kiss was silly; even if she was frightened of loving George, she would not, surely, have made such a how-d'you-do about it, nor pushed him afterwards so resolutely out of her life. She had seen him for a moment glorified, " like heroes—gods—the nonsense of schoolgirls." " Is he not a Demigod, a Narcissus, a Star, the Man i' the Moon ? " as Mrs. Sullen cried to Dorinda of Lord Aimwell seen in church; and Dorinda replied, " I saw him, too, and with an air that shone, methought like rays about his person." Dorinda fell forthwith, and remained, in thrall to love: Lucy, too; and I think not even a " dear, censorious Country-Girl " would have put up such a prolonged and foolish fight, for the Honeychurches were not really snobs.

This pretty and lively piece (it is, by the way, the only story, long or short, by Mr. Forster which ends with lovers in one another's arms anticipating a fine and deathless future) was published in 1908, to the delight of an increasingly admiring public. It had wit, charm, intelligence, poetry, brilliant characterization, and style; in not liking it very much, Mr. Forster was probably in a very small minority. He records that it was " liked by the young, and business men "— an odd combination.

G

# CHAPTER VII

NOVELS were becoming, there seems no doubt, increasingly serious and analytical affairs, as, in Great Britain, the Edwardian age advanced towards the Georgian, and in France the influence of Romain Rolland, Gide, Proust, the Russians, and the introvert psychologists succeeded to the lusty extrovert naturalism of the realists. Barrès' *culte de soi* did not end with the individualist sensationalism of the eighteen-nineties (" *il faut sentir le plus possible en analysant le plus possible* "); it became increasingly analytic, restless, rebellious, at odds with society. The age-old clash between the individual and his environment grew always more vocal and sharp, that clash the consciousness of which is, says Gide, essential for the artist's full development.

In England, fiction took a sociological turn: John Galsworthy earnestly satirized social injustices, cruelties, and the less amiable among wealthy business men, while H. G. Wells, turning restlessly political, followed the humours of *Kipps* with the vehemence of *Anne Veronica* and *The New Machiavelli*. Meanwhile, more introvert novelists,

on either side of the Channel, subjected themselves to the most ardent intensive investigation,
and produced analytical works of the greatest
patience, observation and skill. Henry James had
by 1905 so deftly entangled himself in subtle
implications and delicate gossip by his creatures
about one another, that he could scarcely proceed
at all, for whenever anyone in his novels moved
or spoke such reverberating whispers ran hissing
along the corridors where the gentlemen and
ladies present conversed about those not there.
It was superb, but became immensely stiff going,
and a little airless. With such intense individual
reactions, such intrigues, such beautiful adventures
of mind and heart, there was, anyhow, small room
for those grievances against society at large which
worried another type of writer.

Mr. Forster, meanwhile, following no school,
was developing and enlarging his own field. From
1908-10 he was writing that rich work of delicate
social irony and imaginative individual creation,
*Howards End*. In it he has a little shifted his
ground. Still two worlds, two ways of thought
and life, are at war, but now one is not all truth
and light, the other not all sham and darkness:
both are bad unless they fuse and co-operate.
" Only connect " is the title-page motto, and it is
lack of connection between the two worlds that
atrophies and sterilizes both. On the one side
are ranged the Schlegels, on the other the

Wilcoxes; Margaret Schlegel throws a bridge from one to the other by boldly becoming the second Mrs. Wilcox; the first Mrs. Wilcox by accepting, with calm unintelligence, both worlds.

*Howards End* is Mr. Forster's first fully adult book. It is richly packed with meanings; it has a mellow brilliance, a kind of shot beauty of texture; it runs like a bright, slowish, flickering river, in which different kinds of exciting fish swim and dart among mysterious reedy depths and are observed and described by a highly interested, humane, sympathetic, often compassionate, and usually ironic commentator. The effect is of uncommon beauty and charm; the fusion of humour, perception, social comedy, witty realism, and soaring moral idealism, weaves a rare, captivating, almost hypnotic spell ; and many people think it (in spite of the more impressive theme and more serious technique of *A Passage to India*) Mr. Forster's best book.

If one should be asked what, in brief, it is about, one has a choice of answers. One might say, about two conflicting ways of life and thought, as exemplified in two families. Or about the importance of connecting one thing with another, cause and effect. Or about the outer world of newspapers and golf, empire-building, business and politics, as against the inner world of ideas and of personal relationships. Or about the importance of knowing oneself, of learning to say " I." So much is it about this that Barrès' words from *Le Culte de Moi* might aptly have been taken for one of its mottoes—" *La force de l'intelligence et de la sensibilité appartient à ceux-la seuls qui vivent dans un contact sincère avec leur moi.*" As Helen Schlegel put it,

> " ' There are two kinds of people—our kind, who live straight from the middle of their heads, and the other kind who can't, because their heads have no middles. They can't say " I." They *aren't,* in fact. . . . No superman ever said " I want," because " I want " must lead to the question, " Who am I ? " and so to Pity and to Justice. He only says " want." " Want Europe," if he's Napoleon ; " want wives," if he's Bluebeard ; " want Botticelli," if he's Pierpont Morgan. Never the " I " ; and if you could pierce through him, you'd find panic and emptiness in the middle.' "

Or, if you like, it is about a charming and cultured family, half German and half English, living in London that charming and cultured life that such people could live before the Great Catastrophe trampled their gardens down; and having contacts, entertaining, interesting, bewildering or distressing, with persons outside, such as poor clerks and rich business men. It is (whichever you prefer) a comedy of manners, a complicated interplay of relationships, a tragedy where economic and social factors rather than passions spin the plot, a philosophic morality, the story of a battle of ideas, or of a battle between London and country, a story about a house in Hertfordshire,

where people came and went and lived and died.
A story about people so different, so opposed,
that, if they do not love they must hate; or about
the growth and change in human life. It is so full
and rich, so various and discursive a book that it
can be about almost anything you please, so long
as you admit that it is first about human beings,
their characters, manners, environment, and relationships. In it Mr. Forster emerges as a first-rate
artist of people. There is no failure in his gallery
here. He can paint precisely and bring to quick,
speaking life people from almost every kind of
world. He does not stick to the bourgeoisie, the
intellectuals, the cultured, or the well-to-do. He
can do a drab little insurance clerk and bring him
brilliantly and sympathetically off; he can do the
clerk's wife, a stout, three-parts imbecile, and
practically inarticulate tart; the conversation, if
such it can be called, between these two is, so far
as one can guess, flawless. Apparently it is not
easy to render convincingly the conversation of
prostitutes, for many novelists, in all languages,
have tried and failed, attributing to the members
of this ancient profession, who must nevertheless
be familiar to some of them, a simple romantic
eloquence which may be theirs, but which cannot
convince. Mr. Forster digs up the inarticulate
Jackie from his imagination and sets her solidly
before us, as easily as he musters the Wilcox or
the Schlegel tribes.

Indeed, in foolish ladies he runs always a particularly fine line. To be sure, foolish ladies seem
easier than wise ones, or than foolish gentlemen:
many novelists have been at their best with them;
I suppose that they greatly abound, and that their
folly is excessively apparent. Mrs. Bennett, Lady
Bertram, Miss Bates, Melanctha, Madelon, Mrs.
Malaprop, Lydia Languish, are easier than Elizabeth Bennett, Anne Elliot, Beatrice, Portia,
Cordelia, Electra, or Becky Sharpe; or even than
Osric, Polonius, Mr. Collins, Sir Andrew Ague-
cheek, or Sir Willoughby Patterne. One would
not praise a novelist most for his foolish ladies;
nevertheless, Mr. Forster has of them a fine,
though small, assortment, all different. Only two
are folly unadulterated—the above-described
Jackie, and Dolly Fussel, who married Charles
Wilcox. Dolly is of a higher social status than
Jackie, and is respectable; but she is probably
almost as silly, and, though she talks continuously,
nearly as inarticulate. She is the daughter of an
Indian army officer, is very pretty, and looks silly.
When her husband scolds her, " Tootle, tootle,
playing on the pootle! " she exclaims, suddenly
devoting herself to her baby in its pram. Charles
says, " It's all very well to turn the conversation,"
and the dialogue continues its admirable course.
Dolly is foolish, female, uneducated, good-
natured, and vulgar throughout, and profoundly
suits Charles, who is hard, male, uneducated,

ill-natured and coarse. Dolly's conversations, with her husband, with her father-in-law, with Margaret, are the most brilliantly reproduced patter; there is not a false or redundant chirrup throughout.

The other women in the book are all to be liked. There is Mrs. Munt, the Schlegels' English aunt, one of Mr. Forster's agreeable middle-aged ladies. She has less common sense, sense of humour, and breezy robustness than Mrs. Honeychurch, and more complaisance; she is less good company than that delightful Surrey matron, but still excellent company. She loves and strives to protect her brilliant and erratic nieces from their reckless follies. "The Germans," says she, "are too thorough, and this is all very well sometimes, but at other times it does not do." Hearing the news of the engagement of one of them to an unknown young man in Hertfordshire, off she goes to Hertfordshire to look into it, sworn to discretion, meets by chance at the station Charles, the young man's brother, accepts a lift in his car up to the house, plunges into conversation with him, and explodes Helen's secret. The interview flares into a quarrel, punctuated by calls at shops for parcels. Charles says,

"'Could you possibly lower your voice ? The shopman will hear.'

"*Esprit de classe*—if one may coin the phrase—was strong in Mrs. Munt. She sat quivering while a member of the

lower orders deposited a metal funnel, a saucepan, and a
garden squirt beside the roll of oilcloth.

" ' Right behind ? '

" ' Yes, sir.' And the lower orders vanished in a cloud of
dust."

## The quarrel resumes.

" They played the game of capping families, a round of
which is always played when love would unite two members
of our race. But they played it with unusual vigour, stating in
so many words that Schlegels were better than Wilcoxes,
Wilcoxes than Schlegels. They flung decency aside. The man
was young, the woman deeply stirred ; in both a vein of
coarseness was latent. Their quarrel was no more surprising
than are most quarrels—inevitable at the time, incredible
afterwards."

Having by her affectionate imprudence made
a complete and noisy mess of what would otherwise have been a minor incident quietly tidied away
and buried almost as soon as occurring, Aunt
Juley thinks, throughout her life, " The one time
I really did help Emily's girls was over the
Wilcox business."

But Aunt Juley is charming, kindly, honest,
and to be loved.

Mrs. Wilcox too is kind and honest: Mr.
Forster and Margaret will have it that she is a
great deal more. Margaret feels that she herself
and the others

" are only fragments of that woman's mind. She knows everything. She is everything. She is the house and the tree that

leans over it. . . . She knew about realities. She knew when people were in love, though she was not in the room."

Again,

" She seemed to belong . . . to the house, and to the tree that overshadowed it. One knew that she worshipped the past, and that the instinctive wisdom the past can alone bestow had descended upon her."

She belongs to Howards End, to her ancestors and to the quiet countryside they have for centuries farmed, to the unpretending house, its garden, paddock and hay-fields; she is the country. She is a bore at a lunch party, her remarks are commonplace, often stupid; she thinks it " wiser to leave action and discussion to men "; clever talk alarms her; " she was not intellectual, nor even alert, and it was odd that, all the same, she should give the idea of greatness."

For Margaret, she bridges the gap between seen and unseen, between two worlds; her spirit, in life and after death, brooded gently and serenely over Howards End. We are told nothing that she thought or felt, and Margaret is probably too enthusiastic about her. She may have been much more than a good, kind, simple, country-loving, rather dull woman; but the only evidence for it is Margaret's belief; and Margaret is given to generous enthusiasms.

Margaret herself is the book's centre. She is one of the most actual and realizable of twentieth-century heroines.

"Not beautiful, not supremely brilliant, but filled with something that took the place of both qualities—something best described as a profound vivacity, a continual and sincere response to all that she encountered in her path through life——"

Margaret has most of the attributes that please civilized women in one another. Beauty, merely feminine charm, single-track emotion, biological urge—these qualities, so confusing and swamping to personality and character, so much the stock-in-trade of the heroine-maker, in Margaret Schlegel scarcely exist; in consequence we see her as an individual, with mind, heart, intelligence, sympathies, theories, and ideas. She grows and develops, blunders and advances, she has theories about life, which she tries to follow herself and somewhat vociferously to preach to others. She is delightful, adventurous, erratic, at once a cultured highbrow, a moral enthusiast, a social idealist, a witty talker, and a nice, sympathetic, sensible woman. If we are fortunate, we have known Margaret Schlegels, who are, however, now older by twenty or thirty years. Do such girls still exist, in a young womanhood grown perhaps more primitively sex-conscious, more biologically the feminine creature, than in the brief period of experimental civilization before the great European catastrophe so barbarously upset us all, making fools of idealists, theorists, and those who believed that life was slowly advancing out of the jungle into some more urbane civility? It is possible that, together with such vain fond hopes, the Margaret Schlegels have gone under; or rather that Margaret, then in the twenties, is now fifty, and that the young women who have taken her place are of different, more primitive, perhaps tougher fibre, their bodies, minds and lives set more consciously to fulfil life's simpler destinies; a certain epicene and civil fineness blunted, many-sided intelligence and response perhaps forced into narrower and more urgent channels, the individual more often submerged, swimming in shoals on the biological tide.

Be this as it may, Margaret Schlegel in the year 1910 was an authentic young woman in the twenties, a member of the cultured London bourgeoisie, intelligentsia, intellectuals (or whatever foreign alias we cautiously select, as if none of them quite fitted, for the English professional classes). She and her younger sister and brother were on their father's side German (the old intellectual, idealist, philosophical German type, now in exile or prison), on their mother's of the English family of their aunt Juley, which seems improbable and appears to have left on them little mark. They were sociable, musical, they filled their house with people whom they liked, they even attended public meetings.

" In their own fashion they cared deeply about politics, though not as politicians would have us care ; they desired that public life should mirror whatever is good in the life within. Temperance, tolerance, and sexual equality were intelligible cries to them ; whereas they did not follow our Forward Policy in Thibet with the keen attention that it merits, and would at times dismiss the whole British Empire with a puzzled, if reverent, sigh. Not out of them are the shows of history erected ; the world would be a grey, blood-less place were it composed entirely of Miss Schlegels. But the world being what it is, perhaps they shine out of it like stars."

Politics ; interest in the relation of public to private life ; tolerance ; sexual equality ; profound and vivacious response to everything and everyone encountered ; intellectual ardour and integrity ; unceasing efforts to understand the world, other people, and herself: these are not the usual equip-ments of a heroine, and, thus listed, they sound a little priggish, blue-stocking, and old-fashioned. Margaret tried to see life whole.

" It is impossible to see modern life steadily and see it whole, and she had chosen to see it whole.  Mr. Wilcox saw steadily."

From page 161 on (there are 343 pages altogether) Margaret loves Mr. Wilcox ; but love does not engulf her, she continues to choose to see life whole, even after marriage. She sees through Henry and loves him still—" loved him with too clear a vision to fear his cloudiness."

" The more she let herself love him, the more chance was there that he would set his soul in order. . . . Whether he droned trivialities, as to-day, or sprang kisses on her in the twilight, she could pardon him, she could respond."

" Set his soul in order." Here is Margaret's eager evangelism, that through all vicissitudes pursues the souls of others and herself, endeavouring, for the sake of the general clarification of the human muddle, to tidy them up. Her own she does set in comparative order; Henry's, which is in a shocking mess, she wrestles with, with the hopefulness of the born spring-cleaner, and apparently in the end with some success. Helen's soul has its own erratic career, but Margaret lays on it from time to time a restraining hand; her brother Tibby's is all his own, and she can only give it an indulgent elder-sisterly smile. In the unhappy, muddled soul of Leonard Bast, the clerk, both sisters take a sympathetic interest. " Such a muddle of a man, and yet so worth pulling through. I like him extraordinarily," says Helen. Efforts to pull poor Leonard through end in his financial ruin, disgrace, and finally death. But this is because the efforts are, for the most part, made by the wild and injudicious Helen; Margaret pulls people much better through than that.

Let me not, for a moment, give the impression that Margaret is a prig. On the contrary, this ardent apostle of life is full of eager and generous humility. She dislikes muddle and cant, she hopes for a clear and decent human life, she has ideals, tempered by the salt of ironic perception of things and people as they are.

Helen, on the other hand, has the ideals without

the perception. Helen is a visionary, a reckless extremist; Helen is unbalanced, a balloon without the string that moors Margaret to earth. So she soars up into the stratosphere, pursuing an erratic course among the stars, crashing to earth every now and then with disastrous results to herself and others. She reacts violently and excessively. Attracted for a moment to the Wilcox ideal, the efficient business extrovert life, where things get done and ideals go for nothing, she loves for a few hours a Wilcox young man; they kiss in a garden at dusk. By next morning both have out-lived the transient moment; the young man is in a shamefaced panic, the girl, seeing it, " knew that it would never do—never." Panic and emptiness was what she saw in Paul, and in all the crumbling façade of the Wilcox outer life.

> " I remember Paul at breakfast. I shall never forget him. He had nothing to fall back on. I know that personal relations are the real life, for ever and ever."

From this chance collision Helen reacts further and further as the years go on, towards the inner, the unseen life. Margaret can like the Wilcoxes.

> " She desired to protect them, and often felt that they could protect her, excelling where she was deficient. Once past the rocks of emotion, they knew so well what to do, whom to send for ; their hands were on all the ropes, they had grit as well as grittiness, and she valued grit enormously. They led a life that she could not attain to—the outer life of ' telegrams and anger '

which had detonated when Helen and Paul had touched in June, and had detonated again the other week. To Margaret this life was to remain a real force. She could not despise it, as Helen and Tibby affected to do. It fostered such virtues as neatness, decision, and obedience, virtues of the second rank, no doubt, but they have formed our civilisation. They form character, too ; Margaret could not doubt it : they keep the soul from becoming sloppy. How dare Schlegels despise Wilcoxes, when it takes all sorts to make a world ?

" ' Don't brood too much,' she wrote to Helen, ' on the superiority of the unseen to the seen. It's true, but to brood on it is medieval. Our business is not to contrast the two, but to reconcile them.'

" Helen replied that she had no intention of brooding on such a dull subject."

Helen, a girl of high spirits, is enjoying herself abroad. At the same time, she continues, if not to brood on the dull subject, to set her life to its theme, until her flight from actuality carries her into the brief and desperate (and I think improbable) embrace with Leonard Bast, and her subsequent flight from her family and friends into continental maternity. Or so she intends. In point of fact Margaret steps in, takes hold of the situation, and makes a home both for her and for Henry Wilcox, bringing them together, reconciling the two extremes, bridging the two worlds. In so far as one person can make this bridge, Margaret does so.

The book ends on hope. Helen and Henry have learnt to get on together; Helen is steadier, Henry less muddled; they are living at Howards

End, and the hay-crop will be good. Helen, who could never have been an enthusiastic wife, is an enthusiastic mother; Margaret, who does not want children, is the perfect wife. " To have no illusions, and yet to love—what stronger surety can a woman find ? "

As to Helen, a question remains. Would she really (Edwardian young woman as she was) have spent the night with Leonard Bast ? Edwardian young women of the upper middle classes very rarely, it may be recalled, spent such nights as that, though doubtless more often than was supposed. Helen was not in love; she was moved by pity for Leonard and anger against the social system and against Henry Wilcox who had joined to ruin him. Leonard's wife was sleeping intoxicated upstairs. Helen loved the absolute: Leonard was absolutely ruined. He, and her relations with him, were part of her reaction from the Wilcoxes and the business mind.

" Right up to the end we were Mr. Bast and Miss Schlegel. . . . Oh Meg, the little that is known about these things."

The affair is possible: all the same, one does not quite believe in it. The episode has about it a flavour of device, of contrived drama; it is too sudden and too odd; we are not led skilfully towards it; we feel that these people, whom we thought we knew, have betrayed our confidence, have become two other people. To be sure, this

H

is just what people whom we know in life sometimes do, but art is different, art has a compulsion
that life has not to make the strange natural. The
criticism does, I think, remain valid. As an old
lady put it on first reading *Howards End*, " I
don't think Helen would have forgotten herself
so with that young Mr. Bast." Nor, perhaps,
would young Mr. Bast have forgotten himself so
with Helen. To forget themselves and what they
are really like is one of the things that people in
novels should try and remember not to do.

Apart from this, Helen is vividly realized and
true. She represents a point of view that Mr.
Forster needed for the thesis of his book, and
clothes it in bright, firm flesh and blood. She is at
once a cheerful girl chattering nonsense, a storm-
ing theorist in revolt against the world's injustice,
an eager adventuress swallowing life in pleasant
gulps, and a soaring idealist who forgets the known
earth. One test of her success as an individual
creation is that, though the Schlegel sisters were
alike, bred in the same atmosphere and ideas, no
sentence uttered throughout the book by either
could be mistaken for the other's. Helen takes her
place in Mr. Forster's gallery of heroines as the
most heady and vivacious. Lucy Honeychurch
would have been rattled and bothered by both
Schlegels, and have thought them clever and a little
queer; Agnes Pembroke would, of course, have
hated and feared them, for they read books and

discussed ideas;     Adela Quested would have
found their pace much too quick for her slow,
honest, persevering mind.  They seem to represent a fresh stage in their maker's experience of
life, a stage from which he could tackle women
as freely, as many-sidedly, as much without
puzzlement or caution, as he could tackle men;
that is to say, he could tackle their minds as well
as their emotions.  It is a stage at which few male
novelists have arrived at all;  *mutatis mutandis*,
as few females.  A certain sexless, or epicene,
quality in genius seems to be required for it.

As to the male characters, what a book, in
which the æsthetic Tibby Schlegel so agreeably
and so comically exists side by side with the
philistine Wilcoxes, and the two equally come off !
Tibby is the cultured undergraduate;  his indiffer-
ence to people, his scholarly seclusion of mind, his
under-vitalized emotions, make him the perfect
foil to the robust lowbrow Wilcoxes, whom Mr.
Forster understands equally.  When Charles
Wilcox went to see Tibby, " their interview was
short and absurd.  They had nothing in common
but the English language, and tried by its help
to express what neither of them understood."

Highbrow and lowbrow met on one point:
neither was interested in human beings, or in personal relations.  Tibby

" had never been interested in human beings, for which one
must blame him, but he had had rather too much of them at

Wickham Place. Just as some people cease to attend when
books are mentioned, so Tibby's attention wandered when
' personal relations ' came under discussion. . . . At Oxford
he had learned to say that the importance of human beings has
been vastly over-rated by specialists."

The Wilcoxes, of course, definitely did not like
human beings; they were suspicious of them;
they always wondered what the people they encountered wanted to get out of them. It made
them ill-mannered; perhaps more ill-mannered
than is likely. They hurt the feelings of old friends
(low-class) by returning presents which they
thought too valuable to receive from them; they
insulted the aunts of girls staying with them;
they were intolerably rude to people like the
Schlegels. That is, the younger generation. Mr.
Wilcox is better-mannered, and convinces more.
It looks like Mr. Forster's dislike of Charles, Paul
and Evie having led him a little too far, causing
him to make aggressive boors and churls of those
who would have shown, probably, if encountered
by us, a less pronounced and better concealed
boorishness and churlishness. As with Gerald
Dawes, Mr. Forster's sympathy has been defeated
by this hard churlishness. Still, he was older when
he came to them, and drew them far better; no
doubt but what they are alive, though rude. One
might meet Charles and Evie at a country tennis or
golf club; Paul, more likely, in English clubs in
Nigeria. They are certainly not " saved." Yet

they do not really represent the forces of darkness, only those of stupidity, philistinism, insensitiveness, and suspicion.

Mr. Wilcox senior is a nobler character. He has the business mind; he is efficient, competent, unimaginative, practically clear-headed, intellectually and spiritually muddled, uncivilized, a manly man, with firm theories about women, politics, the Empire, the social fabric. He is concerned wholly with the outer life; the inner is to him an unsounded and uncharted sea. From boyhood he has neglected his soul.

> " ' I am not a fellow who bothers about my own inside.' Outwardly he was cheerful, reliable, and brave ; but within, all had reverted to chaos, ruled, so far as it was ruled at all, by an incomplete asceticism. Whether as boy, husband, or widower, he had always held the sneaking belief that bodily passion is bad, a belief that is only desirable when it is held passionately."

Illogical, obtuse, and not well educated, he cannot connect cause and effect, his own actions with the havoc they have wrought, his own sins with the same sins in other people. He cannot connect the prose in him with the passion, therefore his love seems to the analytical Margaret a cloudy and muddled business. His first kiss after their engagement displeases Margaret.

> " It was so isolated. Nothing in their previous conversation had heralded it, and, worse, still, no tenderness had ensued. If a man cannot lead up to passion, he can at all events lead down

from it, and she had hoped, after her complaisance, for some interchange of gentle words. But he had hurried away as if ashamed, and for an instant she was reminded of Helen and Paul."

Further, Henry lacks exactitude of thought, and therefore honesty.

" The breezy Wilcox manner, though genuine, lacked the clearness of vision that is imperative for truth. When Henry lived in Ducie Street, he remembered the mews ; when he tried to let, he forgot it ; and if anyone had remarked that the mews must be either there or not, he would have felt annoyed, and afterwards have found some opportunity of stigmatizing the speaker as academic. So does my grocer stigmatize me when I complain of the quality of his sultanas, and he answers in one breath that they are the best sultanas, and how can I expect the best sultanas at that price ? It is a flaw inherent in the business mind, and Margaret may do well to be tender to it, considering all that the business mind has done for England."

He has no insight or self-analysis.

" Man is an odd, sad creature as yet, intent on pilfering the earth, and heedless of the growths within himself. He cannot be bored about psychology. . . . He cannot be bothered to digest his own soul."

Such was Mr. Wilcox: and it would seem odd, were such attractions ever odd, that he should have been attracted by the imaginative, psychological, theoretical, soul-analysing, eager specialist in life, Margaret Schlegel, who had neither beauty nor early youth to snare his senses. One would suppose that she would have been, as she was and remained to his children, the kind of woman for whom he had no use at all, and that what his son Charles called her " artistic beastliness " would have kept him in a state of permanent disgust. But love is strange, and the desires of man incalculable. Of woman, too; for Margaret loved Henry, even liked him. We understand that, besides being touched and pleased and amused by the strange ways of this efficient man of business and of middle age, she discerned in his soul something that it would one day become, when she had got to work on its muddle, and done a little digging and weeding (and it must be remembered that this kind of digging and weeding was a hobby of hers). Was she right ? One gathers, in the last pages, that such was the case. We see a Henry broken by trouble, but grown tender and generous and truthful; the gaps in his spiritual equipment seem to be bridged, and Margaret has got him where she wants him. He has achieved the feat so difficult to persons in novels—he has become perceptibly a nicer person, without shock to our sense of probability. His children appear to be unchanged; also, fortunately, his daughter-in-law, the matchless Dolly, who stays the course to the last; to leave its foolish ranges is a thing her soul will never, we may be sure, do. The sons and daughter remain (if we may speak also for Charles, who lies in prison, so that we cannot observe him at close quarters) what they were, hard, rude, self-assertive, vulgar and ignoble. Charles will, we feel, emerge further soured and embittered, a graceless, bewildered, resentful and inarticulate churl; he will probably, we think, live abroad, not among foreigners, whom he always sees through, but somewhere in the Empire, like Paul.

If the Wilcoxes are off the footpath on which walk the people of the Schlegels' own world, Leonard Bast, the unhappy, culture-pursuing young clerk, is still farther from it. Leonard is not educated; he is under-vitalized and sad, with the desperate courage and suspicion of those who walk on the edge of the abyss of poverty. He has his pride.

> " ' If a woman's in trouble ' (he says) ' I don't leave her in the lurch. That's not my street. No, thank you.
> " ' I'll tell you another thing too. I care a good deal about improving myself by means of Literature and Art, and so getting a wider outlook. For instance, when you came in I was reading Ruskin's *Stones of Venice*. I don't say this to boast but just to show you the kind of man I am. I can tell you, I enjoyed that classical concert this afternoon.' "

He will not be patronised by the rich; he is suspicious, and always on guard. He has nobility, and refuses, though ruined, money from Helen. Mr. Forster introduces him to us with sympathy; he represents the half-submerged whom the rich plunder and oppress. But he is kept in proportion, he remains (like Kipps) a naïf and half-literate youth, pathetic, sensitive, ingenuous, badged with the inglorious genteelisms of his class. Whether he and one of the Miss Schlegels, so much by him admired, respected, and envied for their unattainable culture, would have become sudden lovers for a night, has already been questioned. But it does not affect our estimate of Leonard: it seems merely a sudden and not unreasonable demand made on him by his friend and patron Mr. Forster, that his story may be worked out according to plan. Leonard, obliging and loyal, in this as in other matters does his best, allowing himself to be discredited, ruined, even killed, in the service of his friends.

According to plan. For it is part of the book's plan, this flying of Helen to the extreme limits of pity and revolt. " I mean to be thorough," she tells Margaret, " because thoroughness is easy. . . . Unreality and mystery begin as soon as one touches the body." So she turns sharply from the visible, to pursue reality and the absolute, and, in the pursuit, we are meant to understand, takes Leonard in her stride.

Margaret felt her unbalanced, and Margaret was right. Further, by any reckoning Helen's adventure with Leonard was an excursion into the realm of the visible, the physical, and not logically a part of her quest for the absolute. It seems simpler to take it as a lapse from that quest, a slip, when at high tension, into an easy primeval heritage. That Mr. Forster seems to explain it otherwise seems due to his theoretic, analytic method of plot-construction. The naturalistic story-teller, telling his tale of occurrences and people, makes things happen in illogical sequence, without meaning or purpose, though he may moralize about them and spin of them a plot of events—love, hate, death, and what not. The theoretic story-teller, telling his tale of ideas and of life rationalized as he sees it, makes things happen in a pattern, and spins of them a plot of notions. There are no false stitches in his pattern of life. The harmony of the lights and shades and colours in it that gives us pleasure holds also a danger: the design may have arranged them rather than they the design. Such arranging is seldom noticeable in a writer so exquisitely skilled as Mr. Forster, with his gift for making everyone act and speak in character; but one feels the weaver at work; it is the more interesting method, and the resultant pattern is more attractive, since it has meaning and a soul. One method produces an unmeaning procession, the other a fine speculative rationalized design. And when, laying down the book, you come to think what has been its story, you do not say, it is the story of some people, Schlegels, Wilcoxes, Basts, of how they lived and loved and talked and died, and of a house called Howards End: you say, it is the story of the relation between the visible and the invisible, the actual and the ideal, the outer life and the inner, and of the reconciling of these by someone who understood and valued both. That is the real plot; that, and the supremacy of personal relationships.

" It is private life that holds out the mirror to infinity; personal intercourse, and that alone, that ever hints at personality beyond our daily vision."

This emphasis on personal relationships as the key to life is a new emphasis, perhaps experimental. Active minds are looking always for this key or that; hoping vainly to simplify the answer to the odd riddle with which we are posed. Some have said, the key is the love of God; some the love of lovers; some the love of humankind; some the quest for beauty; some the knowledge of the earth; some the desires of the body; some the finding of the mean; some the creation of a good and prosperous society; some the training of the soul. Mr. Forster has experimented now with one key, now with another. In his earlier books, he seems to make truth and directness the key. In *Where Angels Fear to Tread*, the contrast is between the direct, pagan joy in life, and drab conventional propriety. In *The Longest Journey* it is between honesty and muddled meanness; in *A Room With a View* between real feeling and pretended; the darkness is the darkness of sham. " Perhaps," he says, "there is never any contest between love and duty; the contest lay between the real and the pretended."

But in *Howards End* the darkness is that of inhuman depersonalization, the refusal to accept the implications of personal intercourse. Personality is the key. Margaret's " conclusion was that any human being lies nearer to the unseen than any organization, and from this she never varied." The Wilcoxes scarcely recognize human personality; they do not respect it, nor desire intimacy either with their own or with that of others. They ignore and deplore it. Family affection they know (a little irritably) and sex desire (a little shamefaced); with these, their tribute to the personal ends. (Did any of them have intimate friends ? Probably not.) But with no vague affection, divorced from its personal implications, will Margaret have any truck.

Why is the book called *Howards End* ? Not because this was a house in Hertfordshire where the story begins and ends, and where the fortunes of the actors are largely decided; but because it stands, for Mr. Forster, for the stability and privacy of the personal life, as contrasted with the vast, impersonal muddle of the great towns which are spreading octopus arms over England.

" The graver sides of life, the deaths, the partings, the yearnings for love, have their deepest expression in the heart of the fields. . . . In these English farms, if anywhere, one might see life steadily and see it whole, group in one vision its transitoriness and its eternal youth, connect—connect without bitterness until all men are brothers."

Untrue, of course. Nowhere is there less connection, more bitterness, less brotherliness, less vision of life steady and life whole, than there may be in the quiet country places; and life, death, partings and yearnings are as sharply and deeply felt in towns as in villages, since in both it depends on the sensibility of the feeler. But Mr. Forster is giving the musings of Margaret, who has come down from London to the country for the day and, like other London visitors, romanticizes, as she has romanticized that enigmatic country-woman, Mrs. Wilcox. After living a year at Howards End, she perhaps amended her view, occupied as she was in summer with fears lest the well should give out, in winter lest the pipes should freeze, in westerly gales lest the elm should blow down, in hay-time having to keep the windows shut against Henry's hay-fever, all the year round, probably, having difficulties with the neighbours and the servants on account of Helen's baby. Such rural apprehensions leave the less space in the soul for vision, for connecting, for universal brotherliness, and for seeing life either steadily or whole, and Margaret was a practical woman, Martha as well as Mary.

Still, there it is. The hay-field is being cut by Tom's father from the farm; cutters and hay-makers will be all known by name to Margaret;

she will go and see their wives, know about their children's births and ailments; when someone in the village dies, she will send flowers to brighten their graves. Howards End *is* more personal in its relationships than London. Personal relationships for ever and ever, Amen; on this note the novel seems to end.

Is this note, too, of its age, like the occasional period phraseology (" motor " for car, and the rest) and the cultured charm of the pre-war Schlegels? Perhaps. Certainly it would be more difficult to-day to make personal relationships the key to a world so sharply, so menacingly enrolled in mass armies, so widely regimented by mass thought; a world in which the worst dangers that threaten are mass dangers, a world in which we have to (as Dr. Johnson resented people doing) " make a rout about universal liberty," and try to free people in herds. Mr. Forster was later to join in the rout about general liberty: he was to move out of and beyond this experimental view of the solution of human problems, and to concern himself with wider and more public relationships.

Meanwhile, *Howards End* stands as a delicate and exquisitely wrought monument to an age when liberty, equality and fraternity were not absurd cries, when the world was not in so perilously catastrophic a state that to pursue art, grace, elegance and wit savoured of lack of public spirit, when culture was something other to writers than the negation of Fascism, and intellectual liberty was a personal rather than a political aim.

It had, of course, a great reception. In addition to having all the literary graces, wit, irony, delicate distinction of style and thought, it has the exciting readability that does not always accompany these; it is the novel of the born novelist, and has that zest. You do not want to miss a word while reading it; no one that I know of ever has. It is the kind of novel whose characters are real to its readers, who follow their courses with the most breathless and goggle-eyed attention.

# CHAPTER VIII

AFTER *Howards End* the restless interval which often follows the finishing of a major work seems to have supervened; the interval during which the question " What next ? " puts itself rather with a pleasant largeness than with immediacy; creativeness, temporarily satisfied, is asking " What will it entertain me to do next ? " and leisurely ambles over wide fields, here experimenting, there rejecting.

At the end of 1910, there are experimental notes for a novel which never got written: all novelists will recognize the hopeful note.

> " To deal with country life, and possibly Paris. Plenty of young men and children in it, and adventure. If possible, pity and thought. But no love-making. . . . Am sketching a family—father a Tory candidate, a barrister, moderate, sensible, generally kind ; lets his children go loose, but expects them to enter their class without difficulty later. Eldest son—Neville—at Oxford ; second Jocelyn, the hero ; two girls, fourteen and thirteen, and perhaps another boy. A step-mother, quiet and beautiful, who accentuates the father's faults. And an old boot-boy now at the Swindon works, and his two brothers, one a choirboy in a Cathedral. . . ."

An enormous and promising cast: one would like to have seen it in action. But it is not perhaps surprising that its would-be producer should have made the brief entry a few days later, " Tired."

The family, young men and children, boot-boy and choirboy, adventure, pity and thought and all, seem to have been left at that, attractive shades haunting Swindon and possibly Paris; it seems a great pity, and I do not feel that we shall ever get them now, their day is past, poor pre-war ghosts. Abortive, too, unfortunately, was *Arctic Summer*, a novel which was to have been about an efficient civil servant.

Instead of bringing these to birth Mr. Forster was in 1911 writing articles, short stories and reviews, what he calls " a bad unpublished play," *The Heart of Bosnia*, and publishing *The Celestial Omnibus*, a collection of six of the stories that had appeared at various dates in various reviews, and have been commented on earlier in this study. After the very contemporary *Howards End*, they struck an odd, different, fantastic note; here again are Pan, fauns, dendrometamorphosis, Greece, and mystic interpenetrations of other worlds with earth's. Not quite the note, one might feel, for 1911, which appears to have been a disturbing year of crisis, a crucial time for world and Empire. Some of us, who were at the time young and thoughtless, may only remember that it was hot; the most glorious summer for bathing,

I

picnics, tennis, and sleeping in the garden that has
ever in our memory occurred. But, looking
through the newspapers of that year, one perceives
that it was a portentous, alarming, quarrelsome,
fussy kind of year, in which political factions
fought like dogs (one would have supposed it
far too warm) and constitutions tottered, except
the British monarchy, which was confirmed and
exalted by being once again crowned, with the
same unstinted approval from the press as that
which we have suffered of late.

> " The crowning of the KING and QUEEN by a free people
> whose confidence and affection they worthily possess is no idle
> ceremony or mere exhibition of pomp got up to exalt indivi-
> duals and tickle the senses of the unthinking mob. It is the
> consecration, by a solemn public act, of the Headship of the
> State, with the glad consent and assistance of all its component
> parts. The CROWN is the link that binds all parts of the Empire
> together. . . . The THRONE unites us all, and the ceremony
> of the CORONATION will once more demonstrate that remarkable
> fact to the world."

Besides the Coronation, there was an Imperial
Conference and a Delhi Durbar. But, alas,

> " in sharp contrast to these stands the baneful political crisis,
> with its deep and bitter spirit of discord. Is it to throw a
> blight, to tarnish the brightness of the CORONATION ? "

The baneful crisis was, it appears, the Introduction of the Parliament Bill, and the Liberal
proposal for abolition or reform of the House
of Lords. Then there was National Health

Insurance, a Railway Strike, women's suffrage riots, and grave dangers to the Peace of Europe— dangers just averted, but still at the end of the year, menacing.

"A year of great events and greater anxieties" (wrote *The Times* at its conclusion). "The Constitution has been so violently attacked that it is no longer the Constitution that we and our fathers had known."

Anarchists and aliens had also been very troublesome in London. 1912 was no better, being noisy with Near Eastern troubles and bitter political battles at home. The Disestablishment of the Church in Wales " inflicts a deep wound on the religious sensibilities of half the country "— (half the country of England, one supposes, as the religious sensibilities of most of the inhabitants of Wales were gratified). The Home Rulers would " break up the United Kingdom and risk a civil war "; all was outrage and confusion; still, " we may hope to escape the general European war."

I refer briefly to the sad and menacing world of those days in order to indicate what kind of oppression of spirit was liable to sadden and frustrate the imaginations of our just-pre-war writers. Even those brighter spots in the darkness, the CORONATION, the EMPIRE CONFERENCE and the DELHI DURBAR, were not, perhaps, calculated to lighten the heart or please the sensibilities of Mr. Forster. Ironic detachment seemed the only attitude possible for artists; and particularly for an artist who believed that salvation must come through the personal relationships of human beings. In those days, on the whole, writers inclined to cultivate their own gardens more than to-day, when bugles call them continually and insistently to come out and combat world-perils, world-destruction, when scarcely a week may pass without their receiving letters requesting their views on this and that world-pest, inquiring whether or not they think it advisable to co-ordinate the forces of peace and freedom in defence of culture and justice. (I have sometimes wondered whether any writers have the effrontery to reply to this inquiry in the negative.) Before the war, the situation was, as we have seen, both grave and acute (if situations, unlike accents, can be both); Europe was under storm-clouds in act to break, Great Britain was torn by political factions, the Empire looked on in that grave apprehension which is the nearest approach to human weakness that the Empire ever shows. But writers did not disturb themselves so greatly as to-day. It was taken for granted that they all desired peace, freedom, culture, justice, and other felicities, and so no one asked them. Neither, I think, were their views on world affairs considered so important, or so frequently announced to the public.

Of the novelists and poets, large and small, writing in those years, some, of course, concerned

themselves with public affairs, but in the main their
interest was in their own business; I think they
were more selfish. Arnold Bennett was delivering
his long, quiet, sad serial about the long, quiet,
sad lives of persons in midland towns, with refresh-
ing jokes such as *The Card* for relief. H. G. Wells
was now turning his wit and fancy on the life of
Mr. Polly in a Home County village, now flinging
out that brilliant farrago of love and politics,
*The New Machiavelli*, now interpreting the male-
against-female conflict in *Marriage*. Henry James,
declined a little from his zenith, was still delicately
busy ravelling and unravelling polite destinies;
Conrad (considered then, with Hardy, the greatest
English-writing novelist) was dealing in a manner
something similar with nautical ones; John
Galsworthy, his most imposing work over, was
producing minor and less purposeful tales; Mr.
Masefield vivid adventure stories; Anne Sedg-
wick and Charles Marriott delicate psychological studies of human beings (hers were
Jamesian, his Meredithian); Rudyard Kipling
fairy-stories; G. K. Chesterton was throwing his
robust zest for life into fantastic moralities and
metaphysical extravaganzas such as *Manalive* and
*The Ball and the Cross*, which were received with
delight by such readers as disliked both sophistica-
tion and realism and found relief in gay ecclesi-
astical earnestness and brilliant fantastication.
There were, too, the fairy writers, who, like E. M.

Forster in most of his short stories, like Algernon Blackwood, James Stephens, Walter de la Mare, and the just beginning Mr. Forrest Reid, dealt with queer creatures and happenings beyond the rim of our sense life. A school true-blue British, with its mingling of Celtic and Teutonic fancy and delighted absorption of Greek myth. While on the more realistic and less childlike side of the sundering Channel, Jean Christophe unrolled himself piece by piece.

Into this rapidly spreading, rather intimidating sea, shoals and schools (whichever is the correct noun of assembly for them) of young novelists were joyfully and eagerly leaping and swimming— Compton Mackenzie, J. D. Beresford, Hugh Walpole, Frank Swinnerton, Katherine Mansfield, Sheila Kaye-Smith, and a great store more.

But Mr. Forster, after publishing the *Celestial Omnibus* collection, ceased to swim in this increasingly crowded sea; instead of which, he set sail for India.

Of this voyage he wrote twenty-one years later, in his life of Goldsworthy Lowes Dickinson,

" On board were many Anglo-Indians as they were then called. These I have often seen again. The contrast between their clan and our clique was amusing. We were dubbed ' The Professors,' or ' The Salon,' and there was the same little nip of frost in these jests as in the title of ' The Three Graces ' which had been fastened on Dickinson and his school friends at Charterhouse. They recognized that we were gentlemen, sahibs even, and yet there was a barrier. No doubt we did look

queer, and once when we were all four in a row at our tea a
young officer opposite could not keep grave. We played chess
on Sundays, compared Dostoievsky with Tolstoy publicly,
balanced on bollards instead of playing deck games. . . ."

The professors parted in Bombay, taking
separate paths and arriving at separate conclusions,
that here and there were the same. About the
English in India, they were much of a mind.

" Anglo-Indian society," Lowes Dickinson wrote, in a
letter to a friend, " is the devil. . . . We eschew it all we can.
It's the women more than the men that are at fault. There they
are, without their children, with no duties, no charities, with
empty minds and hearts, trying to fill them by playing tennis
and despising the natives. . . . There is no solution of the
problem of governing India. Our presence is a curse both to
them and to us. Our going will be worse. I believe that is the
last word. And *why* can't the races meet ? Simply because the
Indians *bore* the English. *That* is the simple adamantine fact."

" I disagree," says Mr. Forster, " with the
last paragraph." Lowes Dickinson believed that
" *everything* in India will have to be swept away,
except their beautiful dress and their beautiful
brown bodies. . . . But their caste! And their
whole quality of mind. No, it's all wrong. . . .
*Shall* you write a book on India ? *I* shall *not*."

Mr. Forster, who saw India quite differently,
did so. He began it after this first visit, laid it by,
and went on with it after his next visit, about ten
years later.

What India was to him can be read not only in
*A Passage to India*, but in various essays and

fragments scattered about after 1912. It is apparent that, however stirred by the beauties and excitements of the gorgeous and hypnotic East, he kept his head. In the height of the Tagore boom of 1914, for instance, he reviewed Tagore's fairy play, *Chitra*, with all the moderation induced in the intelligent by public fuss, while giving the pretty allegory its due. It was this keeping of the head, this nice mingling of sense and sensibility, which enabled him to draw the Hindus and Mohammedans who are, in *A Passage to India*, so much more vivid, and, at least seemingly, truer, than most of the English. Sympathetic imagination and observation produced Aziz, Hamidullah, Dr. Godbole, and the exquisitely misguided hospitality of the unfortunate brothers in that lovely anecdote *The Suppliant*,* while a sharp sense of beauty and strangeness, and of the character and detail of places, painted the brilliant reports of things seen, such as the aching landscape round the Marabar caves, the hot groves of the pan shrub, and the plains of Ujjain; reports which are like Van Gogh paintings, intense in heat and colour, breathlessly still, febrile and frightening.

But the Indian novel was laid aside. So also, unfortunately, was a projected book on Samuel Butler, and other intentions. For the catastrophe of 1914 crashed in, and writers, like other people, ceased for a while the practice of their profession.

* *Abinger Harvest*

# CHAPTER IX

## GUIDE BOOK

MR. FORSTER spent the war in Alexandria, performing such work as non-combatants perform when their country is at war. Besides this, he wrote a book about Alexandria, of which the first half is a short history, the second an excellent guide. The history is most agreeable reading, full of scholarship, spirit, poetry, humour and prejudices. For prejudices, it would be fairer to say strong tastes and distastes. Mr. Forster, a Hellenist, humanist, and anti-medievalist, admires the ages of Græco-Roman and Ptolemaic Alexandrian culture; he deplores the dark and barbarous centuries that engulfed these, and the fierce orthodoxies, controversies and asceticisms of the Christian church that here had their cradle. " The decline of science coincides with the rise of Christianity," he is always glad to note; coincides, but is, he implies, by no means a coincidence. " The age of inquiry was over, and the age of certainty had begun." And, " It was strange that when science had once gained such triumphs " (as Eratosthenes's measurements of the earth) " mankind should ever have slipped back again into fairy tales and barbarism." His justifiable annoyance at this prolonged barbarism makes him slip into one exaggeration, for, forgetting for a moment Copernicus, he says that the Ptolemaic theory of the universe " supported by all the thunders of the Church " " was adopted by all subsequent astronomers until Galileo." Monks, naturally, are also annoying.

> " By the fourth century, they had gathered into formidable communities, whence they would occasionally make raids on civilization like the Bedouins to-day. . . . The monks had some knowledge of theology and of decorative craft, but they were averse to culture and incapable of thought. Their heroes were St. Ammon who deserted his wife on their wedding eve, or St. Antony, who thought bathing sinful and was consequently carried across the canals of the delta by an angel. From the ranks of such men, the Patriarchs were recruited."

The monks destroyed the worship of Serapis, the Library of Alexandria (" here for four hundred years was the most learned spot on the earth. The Christians wiped it out."); a mob of them tore Hypatia to pieces, and (though Hypatia was not as much in herself as has been sometimes supposed), " with her the Greece that is a spirit expired—the Greece that tried to discover truth and create beauty and that had created Alexandria."

He gives an engaging account of the Arian-Athanasian quarrel: though when he preludes it

with " An age of hatred and misery was approaching," and epitaphs Athanasius with " To us,
living in a secular age, such triumphs appear
remote, and it seems better to die young, like
Alexander the Great, than to drag out this arid
theological Odyssey," his sympathies seem imperfect, his imagination unduly depressed by
classical and humanist distaste, for there was nothing that fourth-century Alexandrians enjoyed
more than a first-class theological scrap, and it is
apparent that a capital time was had by all.

He is more cheerful about the Neo-Platonists,
and has a pleasant account of Plotinus, who

" was probably born at Assiout ; probably ; no one could find
out for certain, because he was reticent about it, saying that
the descent of his soul into his body had been a great misfortune, which he did not desire to discuss. . . . He took part
in a military expedition against Persia, in order to get into
touch with Persian thought (Zoroastrianism) and with Indian
thought (Hinduism, Buddhism). He must have made a queer
soldier and he was certainly an unsuccessful one, for the
expedition suffered defeat, and Plotinus was very nearly
relieved of the disgrace of having a body. Escaping, he made
his way to Rome, and remained there until the end of his life,
lecturing. In spite of his sincerity, he became fashionable, and
the psychic powers that he had acquired not only gained him,
on four occasions, the Mystic vision which was the goal of his
philosophy, but also discovered a necklace which had been
stolen from a rich lady by one of her slaves."

There follows a lucid short account of the
Enneads, and a good section on the growth of the

Christian tree, with its various strange boughs, fruits and flowers, in the richly cultivated spiritual and philosophical soil of Alexandria. Gnosticism, Arianism, Monophysitism, Monothelism, Mohammedanism, orthodox Christianity, are all dealt with in that spirit of detached pleasure which is our modern tribute to the so turbulent disputations of our forebears. For here is that quite unusual thing, a guide-book written by a lover of philosophy and of poetry. It is natural that the heir of Hellenic, the cradle of Alexandrian and Ptolemaic, culture, the ruined tomb of both, the guardian of the learning of the magnificent Mouseion, the temple of Serapis, the kingdom of Cleopatra, the foe and the prey of the " solid but unattractive figure of Rome . . . legal and self-righteous," should fascinate him. It was one of the few kind and happy fortunes of war that placed him here during those deplorable years when most people were so freely and unrewardingly squandered.

The scheme of the book is a very ingenious pretty interweaving of historical and topographical news. In the historical sections, physical events are nicely balanced against intellectual and spiritual, the outer life against the inner, and it comes off both as a history and a guide. There should be—will be, one gathers, in a new edition now preparing—more about medieval and Renaissance Alexandria. One would wish, for instance, to know more of the state of the city described in the twelfth century by Benjamin, the son of Jonas, who saw

> " without the city a great and goodly building, which is reported to have been the College of Aristotle, the Master of Alexandria, wherein there are almost twenty schools . . . and between every one of them were marble pillars. The city itself is excellently built."

Mr. Forster omits Benjamin, but gives some good descriptions by Arabs of the brilliant white city they had taken; and, with a glance at a few sixteenth, seventeenth and eighteenth century travellers, including the " lively but spiteful Mrs. Eliza Fay," passes on to Napoleon, the Battle of the Nile, and Aboukir; and rather odd it is to find him describing in a businesslike manner, with map, a naval engagement and a land campaign. He conducts the city up to its bombardment by the British navy, and pillaging by its own residents, in 1882, and there leaves her, somewhat battered, and with a future before her in which only material prosperity seems assured, for

> " little progress can be discerned in other directions, and neither the Pharos of Sostratus nor the Idylls of Theocritus nor the Enneads of Plotinus are likely to be rivalled in the future. Only the climate, only the north wind and the sea remain as pure as when Menelaus, the first visitor, landed upon Ras-el-Tin three thousand years ago ; and at night the constellation of Berenice's Hair still shines as brightly as when it caught the attention of Conon the astronomer."

There follows the Guide section: it is business-like, entertaining, scholarly, detailed, so far as we know accurate, and has excellent historical plans. Throughout, the vanished ancient city contrives extraordinarily to be apparent to us through the buildings and streets that cover it like a palimpsest. From the Bourse and Cotton Exchange, where

" the howls and cries that may be heard of a morning proceed not from a menagerie, but from the wealthy merchants of Alexandria as they buy and sell,"

we pass to the Rue Rosette,

" the ancient Canopic Way, the central artery of Alexander's town, and under the Ptolemies it was lined from end to end with marble colonnades. . . . At its entrance, right, are : the Caracol Attarine (British Main Guard) ; the Rue de la Gare du Caire, leading to the main railway station ; and the Mohammed Ali Club, the chief in the town—a small temple to Serapis once stood on its site. Here too is Cook's office.

" 100 yds down it is crossed by the Rue Nebi Daniel and by a tramway. Here, in ancient times, was the main crossway of the ancient city—one of the most glorious places in the world (p. 10). Achilles Tatius, a bishop who in A.D. 400 wrote a somewhat foolish and improper novel called Clitophon and Leucippe, thus describes it. . . ."

And so on, the modern and the Arab palimpsesting the ancient all the way. There is an admirable description of the museum, the exhibits cross-referenced to the historical section; and beyond it,

" The Rue Rosette continues, and at last issues from between houses. Here, ever since its foundation, the city has ended ; in Ptolemaic times the Gate of the Sun or Canopic

Gate stood here, in Arab times the Rosetta Gate. The Public
Gardens follow the line of the Arab walls."

The scheme, it will be seen, is at once practical,
imaginative and scholarly; seekers after Greek,
Roman and Ptolemaic antiquity, tombs and cata-
combs, mosques or palaces, the site of the Sera-
peum, or of Cleopatra's Needles, the prehistoric
harbour, Christian monasteries and churches, the
Libyan desert, the office of Mr. Thomas Cook, the
old city of Rosetta, the Cotton Exchange, or the
Pharos Lighthouse, a wonder of the world, are
all conducted, guided and informed, told what
coloured tram to take to get there, and the
archæological and other history of all that they see.
One would wish more guides like this, for the
imagination and mind are fed, fact and detail are
informed by beauty, the ghosts of marble colonnades soar up from tram-lines, the antique world's
great library stands invisible upon its sacred hill,
and the wrecked glory of ancient Alexandria
whispers still in these smart commercial streets.
That is to say, this is a very good guide-book, well
written, well arranged, learned and attractive.
Its interest, and, one supposes, the author's,
culminates in a fine account of the Pharos lighthouse (good plans).

As an example of imagination harnessed to
precision, the poet's playing and reconstructing
mind to the student's painstaking research, the
book is what any tourist wants and too seldom gets.

# CHAPTER X

OUT of the Alexandrian period came also a number of short, witty studies in the antique and the modern, many of which appeared in the *Egyptian Mail*, and some of which were reprinted later in the little book called *Pharos and Pharillon*. Here is the description, largely repeated from the Alexandria Guide, but here expanded, there curtailed, more gaily crisped, embellished and adorned, of the great lighthouse, its construction, its marvels, its myths, its fall. This lovely chapter ends sadly, with

> "The dominant memory in the chaos is now British, for here are some large holes made by Admiral Seymour when he bombarded the Fort in 1882, and laid the basis of our intercourse with modern Egypt."

There is a fragment on Alexander the Great, written with the novelist's lively gift of endearing his characters to his readers.

> "He was never—despite the tuition of Aristotle—a balanced young man, and his old friends complained that in this latter period he sometimes killed them. But to us, who cannot have the perilous honour of his acquaintance, he grows

more lovable now than before. He has caught, by the unintellectual way, a glimpse of something great, if dangerous, and that glimpse came to him first in the recesses of the Siwan Oasis."

The story of Philo's deputation of protest to Caligula shows this gift more clearly, for we all admire Alexander, but the Emperor Caligula is less admirable, less amiable, and yet when, in this lively version of the *legatio ad Gaium*, he leads the earnest and breathless Jewish deputation a dance over his villa, turning on them suddenly to ask " Why don't you eat pork ? " we condone for a moment his notorious excesses, as we condone them when we call to mind his pampered horse, and Mr. Forster and we are pleased with this so extravagant and so luxurious lunatic; pleased, too, with the Deputation, when they reply that, for that matter, some people don't eat lamb; pleased that the Chosen People, in spite of all contretemps and rebuffs, survive and thrive and are to-day not infrequently to be encountered travelling first class. Athanasius, too, pleases us, and Arius, and their ardent and portentous quarrel, even though Athanasius " weaned the Church from her traditions of scholarship and tolerance, the traditions of Clement and Origen."

I think it probable that, had Mr. Forster written an essay even on that fanatical Patriarch, Cyril, or his disagreeable Reader Peter, who led the mob that murdered Hypatia, both might

K

have emerged a little touching, a little humanly silly and nice, and both writer and readers would have begun to sympathize with the fierce clerics. Clement of Alexandria has, of course, no need of such ironic embellishment, for Clement was a learned philosopher as well as a Christian father; Clement could reconcile Greek thought with Christian dogma, clothe the new religion in the amenities of philosophic dress, acknowledge merit in pagan thought, while, instead of being harshly and uncompromisingly ascetic and hell-fire, his treatise on the rich man's salvation

> " handles with delicacy a problem on which business men are naturally sensitive, and arrives at the comforting conclusion that Christ did not mean what he said. One recognizes the wary resident. And when he attacks Paganism he seldom denounces: he mocks, knowing this to be the better way. . . ."

He derided the priests in the idol-temples for their dirt, and neither he nor his hearers foresaw the impending Christian holiness of dirt. There was nothing morose about Clement, and

> " his verdict is that, though the poetry of Hellas is false and its cults absurd or vile, yet its philosophers and grasshoppers possessed a certain measure of divine truth; some of the speculations of Plato, for instance, had been inspired by the Psalms. It is not much of a verdict in the light of modern research; but it is a moderate verdict for a Father; he spares his thunders, he does not exalt asceticism, he is never anti-social."

Clement was, in fact, as we knew already, charming and so needs Mr. Forster's endearing method the less, and deserves and rewards it the more. Not that the fanatical clergy and heretics of history do not also reward irony, as has been shown often enough by those who have recorded them; highly amusing in themselves, they only need one smile more to make them the most droll and delightful of figures. At giving this smile, and making it a pleased, a friendly, almost an affectionate, smile, Mr. Forster is an adept. His fanatics, his simple monks, his earnest and eccentric enthusiasts, take on accents of the gayest social success. They appear nicer, often, than they can have been; and the stories of their lives are simplified by the novelist's foreshortening art to an absurdity far more agreeable than the tediously protracted turbulence and intrigue recorded by historians. The Monophysite monk, Timothy the Cat, for example, in Mr. Forster's account is a charmingly sly intriguer crying " Miaou " in the monastery at night, gibbering and bowing and saying in hollow tones " Consecrate Timothy," then being found on his knees in his cell, all prayer and innocence, two days later to be forcibly consecrated Patriarch by two Monophysite bishops. Then, after the murder of the already existing Patriarch by leading residents, Timothy, " diffident and colloquial, won everyone's heart, and obtained, for some reason or other, the surname of the Cat."

How much less polished and more shameless and violent a careerist he sounds in the pages of Theodore Lector, Mansi and others where

> " creeping at night to the cells of certain ignorant monks, he called to each by name, and on being asked who he was, replied ' I am an angel, sent to warn you to break off communion with Proterius, and to choose Timotheus as bishop.' Collecting a band of turbulent men, he took possession, in the latter part of Lent, of the great Cæsarean church, and was there lawlessly consecrated by only two bishops, who, like himself, had been sentenced to exile. . . ."

After a few days, his adherents murdered Proterius. . . . And so on. It is not so good; we prefer Mr. Forster's Timothy; we like the gay, caressing and titillating candles of comedy to light for us the sawdusty antic by-ways of history.

And to flicker over more recent history also, such as Mrs. Eliza Fay's immortal, spirited, and acid travels about Egypt and the Red Sea, and over the delirious excitement of the modern Alexandrian Cotton Bourse (" Oh, Heaven help us. What is that dreadful noise. Run, run. Has somebody been killed ? " " Do not distress yourself, kind-hearted sir. It is only the merchants of Alexandria, buying cotton.") and the (mostly unrewarded) search for an Alexandrian hashish den.

There are two or three studies in still life—the genteel, modernized Rue Rosette, and the ungenteel, unmodernized, flashing explosion of

March flowers in the solitary limestone country
west of Lake Mariout: a lovely essay in the glory
of brilliant, sudden and transient Egyptian
vegetables. Finally, there is an essay in *Pharos
and Pharillon* on Mr. C. P. Cavafy, the Alexandrian poet, whose sentences in conversation
suggest to us those of Henry James, whose poetry
(in translation) that of a cross between a Greek
anthologist and a Chinese poet of the T'ang
dynasty; it has that elegance, that humour, and
that chime of rueful mortality.

Some of the Alexandrian articles only remain
in the faint grey print and shaggy grey paper of the
*Egyptian Mail* in which they appeared. Through
these hindrances emerge a disorderly Sunday
concert; an idiotic film; some Gippo English;
the foolish Egypt of the photographs; a report of
a first flight; another (reprinted in *Abinger
Harvest*), of an evening entertainment for the
military; this, called *The Scallies*, is funnier than
the poor Scallies themselves can have been, or
ever are; it gives the kind of pleasure that one
gets from attending Scallies and similar diversions
with the right kind of commentating wit at one's
elbow; the wit, ironic, rueful, sympathetic, slant-
ing, which lights Mrs. Eliza Fay's trip to Egypt
to an absurdity much brighter than it enjoys in its
own right.

This wit, having entertained itself with events
and persons picked randomly out of twenty-three

centuries of Alexandrian history, now turned itself on to more various fields, more or less randomly still, led by predilections, aversions, admirations and tastes, and by those chancy fortunes of reviewing which induce often such very improbable contacts.

# CHAPTER XI

IN some of the miscellaneous essays, reviews, and other comments on the world of life and letters which Mr. Forster scattered about various periodicals during the immediately post-war years, one perceives (possibly because one is ready to assume) a new note, a note of greater gravity, sometimes of the bitterness suitable to the embittering occasion. The war years have stalked by, a grim procession, to a grim end; the dust and the war-cries, subsiding a little, leave a bemused world of people looking at each other with a surmise too weary and perplexed to be wild: the cup of victory is lifted in unsteady hands, and over its rim tired, confused, and rather vulgar persons, still in the quarrelsome stage of intoxication, stare foolishly across a littered, crazy and corpse-strewn world at a highly dubious to-morrow. This, which may sound fanciful, is in fact pretty much what many of us felt. I am not insisting that Mr. Forster felt it; Alexandria, India, philosophy, literature and irony may have enabled him to keep his head among the stampeding, futile hatreds and the desolation of the crowding graves. But no one could come through these four years and write just as before, and in point of fact I think no one did. Even the technique of writing (both prose and verse) was altering, becoming sharper, more skilful, more introvert and significant, less romantic. On the one hand, the outward circumstance of trivial speech and action, blandly detailed, was offered us more heavily charged with meaning, as Tchekov's influence spread; on the other, the inward procession of the mind's encounters flowed in meandering streams, a looking-glass to life, after the method begun in England by Dorothy Richardson and followed by James Joyce. In France, the untiringly inquisitive researches of M. Proust after his past combined happily the inward and the outward and the quiet pleasures of unhappy social and emotional entanglements. New graces of style and swiftnesses of thought were brought to the English novel by Virginia Woolf; new allusiveness, irony and ellipsis, and an anti-sweet tang, to poetry by T. S. Eliot; new mirth to the study of the eminent by Lytton Strachey, Philip Guedalla, and Harold Nicolson. Increasingly, we saw ourselves as children of our age, children of unbelief, children of a mocking despair. Not that we had not always seen ourselves as this, for the children of every age do so; in 1907 Mr. Forster had expounded the view to the Working Men's College; and it seems likely that so self-flattering an illusion will never be out of fashion, besides, of many of us it is quite true enough to pass.

I do not know that this view of our age, or any other current influence, greatly worked on Mr. Forster, who retained his previous views of life, with the slightly increased list to port that the reeling storms had induced. The voyage certainly had a more formidable look, the horizon was more greatly obscured, the whole business, always enigmatic, had become an enigma without such solutions as had seemed to offer themselves in the days of *The Longest Journey* and *Howards End*. "O Life, what art thou?" he inquires, in an essay of 1919,* gibing at the clichés of trite and hearty men.

"Life seldom answers this question. But her silence is of little consequence, for schoolmasters and other men of good will are well qualified to answer for her. She is, they inform us, a game. Which game? Bagatelle? No, Life is serious, so not bagatelle, but any game that . . . er . . . is not a game of mere chance; not Baccarat, but Chess; or, in moderation, Bridge; yes, or better still, Football with its goals and healthy open-air atmosphere and its *esprit de corps*; Fate is the umpire and Hope is the ball: hie to the football ground all, all, all.—Thus far and even further the men of good will. Once started on the subject of Life they lose all diffidence, because to them it is ethical. They love discussing what we ought to be instead of what we have to face—reams about conduct and nothing about those agitating apparitions that rise from the ground or fall from the sky. When they say that Life is a game they only mean that some games develop certain qualities, such as heartiness, which they appreciate."

* *Abinger Harvest*

He decides in the end that life is Piquet.

" Think for a moment about Piquet. It is in the first place obviously and overwhelmingly unfair. Fate is dealt, despite skill in discarding, and neither in the rules of play nor in the marking is there the least attempt to redress misfortune or to give the sufferer a fresh chance. The bias is all the other way. Disaster is an additional reason for disaster—culminating in the crowning butchery of Rubicon, where the very bones of the victim are gathered up by the conqueror and flung like sticks upon his bonfire. Yet this savage pastime admits the element of Free Will. It is possible to retard or accelerate Fate. Play, subtle and vigorous play, goes on all the time, though the player is being swept to disaster or victory by causes beyond his control, and it is in the play, rather than the result, that the real interest of the game resides. Another affair, in which all the living and possibly all the dead are engaged, runs on similar lines. Failure or success seem to have been allotted to men by their stars. But they retain the power of wriggling, of fighting with their star or against it, and in the whole universe the only really interesting movement is this wriggle. O Life, thou art Piquet, in fact. A grim relaxation. Still, she might have been Golf."

The view, the sentiments, might be Thomas Hardy's, though the voice could not. It is the mockery of despairing disgust.

Nostalgia, too, has set in. Reviewing a " beautiful book," *Macao et Cosmage*,* which is about happiness on an island, with giraffes and turtles and cataracts and forests, happiness destroyed by a Commandant who landed on the island and introduced the benefits of civilization, introduced

* *Abinger Harvest.*

" l'époque des grandes inventions," Mr. Forster
ends:

> "O wisest of books! What help do you bring after all?
> You only underline the inevitable. As the author remarks,
> 'Enfant, Macao était un sage, mais le gouverneur avait
> raison.' But your scarlet birds, your purple precipices and
> white ponds, are part of a dream from which humanity will
> never awake. In the heart of each man there is contrived, by
> desperate devices, a magical island such as yours. We place it
> in the past or the future for safety, for we dare not locate it in
> the present, because of the Commandant Létambot, who sails
> upon every sea. We call it a memory or a vision to lend it
> solidity, but it is neither really; it is the outcome of our sad-
> ness, and of our disgust with the world that we have made."

Very escapist, to use a vile new unEnglish word,
that Mr. Forster (I have confidence) has never
used, that I have used myself but this once, because I cannot recall the good old English word
that one should use instead (fugitive, is it? Or day-
dreaming?). Anyhow, escape from our disgust
with the world which we had made seemed
necessary to most of us after the war; since then,
I think, a braver, fiercer, nobler, more unselfish,
perhaps less sensitive, generation has grown up,
and " escapist "—(I have not called it a generation
sensitive to words, I think it is too preoccupied
with the urgencies of fact to be this, and there is
perpetual vigorous thrusting from those new
scientific, non-humanist elements in education
which have never cherished words; it says
*escapist*, and God help it, *ideologies*, and thinks

you a pedant to demur)—" escapist," as I was saying, is on its lips a term of the utmost contempt.

Mr. Forster wrote, in 1920, a very pleasant essay on escape. He called it " The Consolations of History,"* and its theme is " we can recover self-confidence by snubbing the dead." " We cannot," he goes on,

> " visit either the great or the rich when they are our contemporaries, but by a fortunate arrangement the palaces of Ujjain and the warehouses of Ormus are open for ever, and we can even behave outrageously in them without being expelled. The King of Ujjain, we announce, is extravagant, the merchants of Ormus unspeakably licentious . . . and sure enough Ormus is a desert now and Ujjain a jungle. Difficult to realize that the past was once the present, and that, transferred to it, one would be just the same little worm as to-day, unimportant, parasitic, nervous, occupied with trifles, unable to go anywhere or alter anything, friendly only with the obscure, and only at ease with the dead. . . . If only the sense of actuality can be lulled—and it sleeps for ever in most historians—there is no passion that cannot be gratified in the past. The past is devoid of all dangers, social and moral, and one can meet with perfect ease not only kings, but people who are even rarer on one's visiting list. We are alluding to courtesans. It is seemly and decent to meditate upon dead courtesans."

Courtesans on the grand scale, as organized in the sixteenth-century Hindu kingdom of Vijayanagar, where all the personable female population accompanied the armies to battle, and, when the soldiers ran away, remained on the field and accrued to the victors.

* *Abinger Harvest.*

> " With existence as it threatens to-day—a draggled mass of
> elderly people and barbed wire—it is agreeable to glance back
> at those enchanted carnages, and to croon over conditions that
> we now subscribe to exterminate. Tight little faces from
> Oxford, fish-shaped faces from Cambridge—we cannot help
> having our dreams. Was life then warm and tremendous ? "

There are, too, the pleasures of moral censure:
" The schoolmaster in each of us awakes, ex-
amines the facts of History, and marks them on
the result of the examination."

Proceeding to do this, Mr. Forster becomes
capricious and perverse: the thought of schoolmasters is apt to make him so.

> " Why was it right of Drake to play bowls when he heard
> the Armada was approaching, but wrong of Charles II to
> catch moths when he heard that the Dutch Fleet had entered
> the Medway ? The answer is ' Because Drake won.' Why
> was it right of Alexander the Great to throw away water
> when his army was perishing, but wrong of Marie Antoinette
> to say ' Let them eat cake ' ? The answer is ' Because Marie
> Antoinette was executed.' "

The answer, in both cases, is, of course, nothing
of the sort: it is that Drake only went on playing
bowls for a minute or two, then got busy about
the Armada, but Charles, we gather, cared nothing
for the Dutch Fleet; it is that Alexander was in-
spired by noble, if foolish, motives, Marie Antoi-
nette by the cruel ignorance of the stupid rich
woman. Her execution is really her only claim on
the schoolmaster's good marks. But Mr. Forster,

carried away by his pleasure in teasing the simple
and smug pedagogues, will make success their
criterion, and does not allude to any of the successful but very-ill-thought-of-by-schoolmasters mas-
sacres and crimes of history. Indeed, one is never
sure that he does justice to the fumbling, blundering, but persevering moral sense of humanity,
which in the long run approves the persecuted
and condemns the persecutors. But how well
this essay ends:

" To pity the dead because they are dead is to experience an
exquisite pleasure. . . . It is half a sensuous delight, half
gratified vanity, and Shakespeare knew what he was about
when he ascribed such a sensation to the fantastical Armado.
They had been laughing at Hector, and Armado, with every
appearance of generosity, exclaims : ' The sweet war-man is
dead and rotten ; sweet chucks, beat not the bones of the
buried ; when he breathed he was a man.' It was his happiest
moment ; he had never felt more certain either that he was
alive himself, or that he was Hector. And it is a happiness that
we can all experience until the sense of actuality breaks in.
Pity wraps the student of the past in an ambrosial cloud, and
washes his limbs with eternal youth. ' Dear dead women with
such hair too,' but not ' I feel chilly and grown old.' That
comes with the awakening.'

This nostalgic fugitivism endeared to him the
eerie undertones in the novels of Mr. Forrest
Reid, with their faintly sinister backgrounds to
commonplace middle-class lives led in North
Ireland, their sense of something round the corner
too lovely or too fearful for mortal eyes: these

equivocal tenebrios are perhaps the Celtic equiva-
lents of Mr. Forster's own outgrown fauns and
dryads and fields without noise: " the world that
is called up is some dark nameless star swimming
in a black remote sky, and the creatures that in-
habit it are phantoms, misty beings without flesh
or blood, but knowing all the grim secrets of the
grave." It sounds like *Wuthering Heights*, but is
Mr. Reid on Poe, and Mr. Forster applies it to
Mr. Reid's own work. The whole appreciation*
(written in 1919) is significant, as expressing a
natural humour of the writer's which, always
present, is often overlaid and pushed aside by other
moods.

Still feeling nostalgic, he turns east, and writes
of mosques (to which he gives higher marks than
to Christian places of worship); of that resourceful
and successful filibuster, Sir Wallis Budge,* who
plundered antiquities from Cairo for the British
Museum (" We part from him with admiration, but
without tenderness, and with an increased determination to rob the British Museum "); of Wil-
frid Blunt,* so detestable to the official and the
nationalist British mind, so noble a figure to the
Oriental, and to the sensitive occidental a brilliant,
lovable, vain and magnificent free-lance. To his
picture of Blunt one may apply his own comment
on Blunt's judgment of Edward VII—" It is as
firm as an eighteenth-century ' character.' And the

* *Abinger Harvest.*

breath of life is added by an imaginative touch, such as only a poet can give." One might add, only a novelist: all these portraits have a delicate and springing life, a round and supple shape, as if some gay and melancholy drama was forming round them, has already formed, but the curtain must be dipped before there is time to have the rest of the cast on and act it out, so down it comes while the protagonist turns his head to address someone or other, and even while he gestures on the lit and amusing stage, he is cut off from view. It is tantalizing, all that life and brightness and comedy in so brief and fleeting a drama.

The reviews of these years are scattered about in various magazines—the *Athenæum*, *Nation*, *New Statesman* (there were more weekly magazines then, and fewer gorged pythons)—*Spectator*, *Daily News*, *Daily Herald* (of which Mr. Forster was for a time literary editor), and are of many kinds of books. Reviews are ephemeral stuff, which is a pity when they have so much grace, style, humour, learning and (if I may use the loathed word without offence) charm as these. They have, too, a human sympathy that delicately and ironically plays over nearly all God's creatures, even over novelists, even over missionaries to the heathen Chinese. It only dries up, or acidulates, when confronted with a headmaster of a Kashmir Mission School, who wrote, it seems, a book about his activities which

" indicates the sort of person who is still trotting about India. The Indian climate has much to answer for, but it can seldom have produced anything quite as odd as *Character Building in Kashmir*—anything quite so noisy, meddlesome, and self-righteous, so heartless and brainless, so full of racial and religious ' swank.' What is the aim of such a book ? As the author himself puts it, ' Qui bono ? ' And why has the C.M.S. published it ? For it is bound to create grave prejudice against their other workers in foreign fields."

And these are perhaps the severest remarks that Mr. Forster has made in public about any of his fellow-creatures, except, many years later, when people had become worse, about Sir Oswald Mosley's Blackshirts; and it is worth noting that the Blackshirts and this missionary are not (apparently) unlike; both believe in coercion of others into the kind of behaviour and opinions that they think correct.

Mr. Forster turns with pleasure to the poetry of the Persian poet Iqbal, with mild regret to " a bad little book " by a Bengali about Bengal village life, with reverence to the autobiography of the father of Rabindranath Tagore, with entertainment to various enterprises in Egypt, and with immense, though critical, enthusiasm, to Mr. Wells's *Outline of History*. He opens his review of the first volume of this with, " It's no good humming and hawing; at least it is, but before the operation begins the following sentence must be penned: A great book." Before proceeding to

L

hum and haw, he has a brilliant commentary on Mr. Wells's method and its effect on some readers—

> " What, after reading the book, is one's main sensation ? Perhaps that it wasn't so much a book as a lecture, delivered by a vigorous, fair-minded and well-informed free-lance. He was assisted by a lantern—its assistance was essential—and bright and clear upon the sheet he projected the misty beginnings of fact. The rocks bubbled and the sea smoked. Presently there was an inter-tidal scum : it was life, trying to move out of the warm water, and subsequent slides showed the various forms it took. A movement also became perceptible among the audience ; one or two of the prehistoric experts, discontented at so much lucidity, withdrew. Man, Neanderthalian, Paleo- and Neo-lithic ; man in Mesopotamia and Egypt ; nomad man ; man in Judæa (more experts go out), in Greece (still more), in India (exeunt the Theosophists), in China (murmurs of ' me no likee '), and in Rome. Over Rome there is a serious disturbance ; the Public School masters rise to protest against the caricature of Julius Cæsar, while the neo-Catholics denounce the belittlement of the Pax Romana and the Latin Thing, and lumber out to drink beer. The lecturer, undeterred by these secessions, describes the origins of Christianity and loses the Anglican section of his flock meanwhile, though the withdrawal is quieter in this case, and due more to bewilderment than wrath. Finally the lights are turned up, and the room seems as full as ever : one can't believe that a single person has left it. Immense applause. The lecturer thanks the lanternist. . . ."

There follows the humming and hawing; Wells, despite his sweep and his grasp and his racy manner, can't create individuals; brilliant with mass movements, he fails with persons; he

is too much annoyed with the ignorance of our
ancestors; he even " notes the uneducated tendencies of the reptiles, who might have averted
extinction had they taken appropriate steps."
Like most scientists, he confuses information with
wisdom, and, though his intelligence is both
subtle and strong, it cannot quite supply his lack
of imagination.   Further, he is an optimist; he
believes in progress, even in a progressing God,
is too often æsthetically blind, and, because of
Napoleon's destructiveness to Europe, can't see
his greatness.   And there should have been fewer
sketches, and more photographs.   " And there
shouldn't have been any fig-leaves: they are contrary to the whole spirit of such a book."   Still, a
great book, " a wonderful achievement, and
nothing in our generation is likely to supersede
it."

    This otherwise admirable criticism seems not
quite fair to Wells's imagination, one of the most
brilliantly lavish and inventive forces of our day;
but Mr. Forster is not invariably quite fair to the
scientific type of mind, as Mr. Wells himself is
never in the least fair to the classical.   Each has
his blind spots; but Mr. Forster's did not obscure
for him the bright bold flashing of the Wellsian
head-lamps as that high-powered car raced,
throttle full out, down our involved and murky
story.   Mr. Forster's admiration and sympathy go
out to the audacious, venturesome and brilliant

achievement, as they go out to Napoleon's or Alexander's essays in putting girdles round the earth; a certain Puckishness in the method as well in the attempt further appeals to him; he is captivated, and applauds a great show.

One of the points about Mr. Forster's reviewing is that, even when least captivated, he is still respectful (except only to the pretentious, the schoolmasters, and the bullies). He is a courteous, considerate and kind reviewer, never a smart Alec. He pays even foolish writers and tedious writers the tribute of trying to understand what they would be at. As if he were a Jain, who believes even the meanest creatures to have souls, and will not crush or destroy them, he handles them with enquiring gentleness, he will smile, even mock, but will not deride, not talk them down.

Here, for instance, is a review headed " To simply feel," and it reviews a volume of verse by the American poet, Mrs. Ella Wheeler Wilcox, and a novel about Burma by someone else. Easy to make fun of Mrs. Wilcox, it has been done, no doubt, by practically all her readers and by many who have never read a line of her; she was, in fact, in her time (now forgotten, I suppose) an Aunt Sally, a cockshy, the poetical equivalent of Mrs. Barclay and Miss Ethel Dell. But Mr. Forster is as gentle as you please.

" Here are delicate subjects, but she approaches them with the confidence of a capacious heart. Thanks to her intense feeling, she has access to Heaven, which proves to be far more unconventional than Dante or any of the Churches have dreamed. . . .

" Mr. Hall is a more skilful writer than Mrs. Wilcox, but his lack of nobility makes him less pleasant reading. . . . Those who imagine that Mrs. Wilcox is mere silliness would do well to glance at *Poems of Problems*—they will find amongst its crudities a real desire to elevate humanity."

And that, one feels, is the decent, kindly line to take with such as Mrs. Wilcox. Of the other writer reviewed in this article Mr. Forster is less tolerant, makes more game; but apparently this author is pretentious, something of a bully and a schoolmaster, and therefore outside the charity even of the near-Jain.

Looking through the other reviews, one finds no contempt; difference of opinion, yes, ironic ragging often, criticism and regret in adequate doses as required, prejudice and unfairness, yes, here and there. As in the case of the Reverend Stopford Brooke (a preacher, a Victorian moralist, a Unitarian clergyman, but not a bully) *à propos* of whose *Naturalism in English Poetry* the reviewer says that " beauty was to him only the fact that got the preacher going." If this is the impression given by *Naturalism in English Poetry*, it must be a much more deplorable book than Mr. Forster says (I have not read it); but one cannot read this clergyman on the early English poetry of North-umbria (with his own renderings into modern English verse) and still think that beauty was to him only that. Again, can it be accurate to dig a great gulf between the nineteenth and twentieth centuries ?

> " We seek the vital from a complication of reasons ; the nineteenth century the moral, and the great gulf between us is fixed mainly on those lines."

One hears shrill, protesting nineteenth-century cries from Shelley, Byron, Emily Brontë, Pater, Oscar Wilde, and feels that these chronological pens for millions of sheep of different breeds are too slick, too little individual, for Mr. Forster, with his creed of individual personalities, and when he makes use of them one suspects that he is merely feeling a little tired, and has momentarily succumbed to the facile falsities beloved of simpler minds, and of minds which lack power to discriminate between one person and the next.

He is more himself when reviewing a book by Mrs. Wharton on the habits of the French: one of these, said she, was that of not eating blackberries; but when Mr. Forster asked two French ladies about this, they replied, " Mais on les mange tout le temps "; and so much for racial generalizations. Reverence, too—

> " May not some Frenchmen be reverent and others not ? There was Racine, and also Voltaire ; there is Claudel, and also Anatole France. The more one shakes a book of this sort, the more its leaves fall out. It has turned from the individual, the only reliable unit, to masses of individuals. . . . Generalizations are sometimes necessary for human intercourse, and

clarity of thought itself becomes impossible without them. But they are the desperate device of our weakness, of our inability to remember the various separate facts that we have encountered : they are horses that gallop us away from the country where we ought to have stopped, and where blackberries are eaten by some of the inhabitants though not by all."

And from centuries in which the moral and the vital are each sought by some but not by all, and into the great gulf that we dig between adjacent periods, where the glibly galloping cavalcade will, we hope, founder and crash, leaving us to explore the ground on foot, with noses nearer to facts.

Of course there is something in it, as in so many of the assertions that sound glib. We can say yes and no to nearly all generalizations, since we are, most of us, afflicted by the doctrine, or the disease, which the Jains, who cultivate it, call *Syàd-vàda*, which means (so they say) saying yes and no equally to all philosophic statements. It is a pleasant and comprehensive disease, and enlarges the sympathies and the credulities, while possibly mushing up the intellect. Mr. Forster has it less than most of us, for he really has some personal beliefs, doctrines and philosophy about the world. He believes, for example, in personal relationships, in individuality, in beauty, in affection, in liberty and in democracy: he disbelieves in nationalism, empires, militarism, catch-words, Christianity, oligarchy, dictatorship, big business, schoolmasters, and a number of other things. I suppose, if you really have syàd-vàda, you must say yes and no to all these things at once.

Mr. Forster, reviewing in the same period Andre Gidé's *Le Prométhée mal enchaîné*, rightly regards M. Gide as a rather indiscriminate yes and no man.

> " Sometimes he is decrying religion and society, sometimes he turns out scented lyrical descriptions of oriental life, sometimes he upholds miracles, titles, and the other trimmings, new and old, that Authority assumes. His outlook is so subtle and personal that he cannot keep long to the paths of other men, nor indeed to his own. He is always veering. . . . Much has been written about his philosophy, but surely the truth is that he has none."

So keen, through nearly all these reviews, is the perception, so delicate and precise the analysis, so imaginative the penetration, so wide the sympathies (here, to name a few only of the reviewed, are Dostoevsky, Tchekov, Conrad, Mr. Waley's Chinese and Japanese poetry, Ethel Smyth, Virginia Woolf, C. M. Doughty, George Birmingham, Elinor Glyn) and often so vivid, amusing and touching the portrait emerging from them of the writer reviewed as well as of his book, that we approach with gratification an article (dated 1920) called *Notes on the English Character*.* An equivocal title, and a somewhat suspicious, inapprehensible topic, about which too much has been written already, and too little of it

* *Abinger Harvest.*

true. But Mr. Forster has earned the right to take such notes, and notes and queries they will be, not dogmas and firm generalizations: " notes," as he says, " on the English character as it has struck a novelist." It might, of course, and does, strike other novelists differently; we are all susceptible to these blows from different angles. It strikes Mr. Forster, for instance, that the English character is essentially middle class, because the middle classes have been the dominant force in our community for so long. There is something in it; but it might equally well strike him that the French character, with its orderly thrift and industry, is essentially middle class. It struck Taine, who disliked us and thought well only of the French, that we were still (1870) grossly carnivorous, warlike, intoxicated savages, and that drunkenness, up to the end of the eighteenth century the main recreation of our higher ranks (one wonders what he made of Horace Walpole, Lord Chesterfield, and Dr. Johnson), was still that of the lower. In fact, we were barbarians, and lacked the sentiment of the beautiful. Our main traits have been drunkenness, gluttony, violence, and religious melancholia— traits not very middle class or public school.

*Second note.* " The heart of the middle classes is the public school system, which is unique, be- cause it was created by the Anglo-Saxon middle classes, and can only flourish where they flourish."

Surely questionable. Can we make an arbitrary cleavage somewhere in the history of our ancient schools, which were created by benefactors largely for poor boys, and have, since several centuries, been the homes of the sons of the aristocracy as well as of the middle classes ? Granted that they have lost their poor-boy's character and been appropriated by the rich, is the stamp now given by them predominantly middle class ? I suppose one might say so, since the aristocracy are fewer in numbers.

However this may be, it is of course accurate to emphasise the great and unique-among-the-nations influence of the public school on the after life.

> " And they go forth into a world that is not entirely composed of public school men or even of Anglo-Saxons, but of men who are as various as the sands of the sea ; into a world of whose richness and subtlety they have no conception. They go forth into it with well-developed bodies, fairly developed minds, and undeveloped hearts. And it is this undeveloped heart that is largely responsible for the difficulties of Englishmen abroad. An undeveloped heart—not a cold one. The difference is important. . . ."

Few hearts, of course, are much developed. But a case might be made for English hearts being softer, mushier, more easily moved to pity and sympathy by misfortune, than many others. We are more readily shocked by pain and misery than some; ours was the first nation to drop torture from its penal code; our hearts throb towards animals (unless we are pursuing them with weapons of destruction) with ardent, if patchy, philozoism; and no race complains with more eloquent conviction of the shocking wrongs inflicted on foreigners by their respective governments. We behave, it is true, to our fellow-humans less cordially than they normally behave elsewhere, and eye them with a warier circumspection than they do almost anywhere outside the Red Indian reserves; nevertheless, one would sooner be stranded in a mess among average English people than among most, for one believes their hearts and pockets to be more touchable than those of many races. Mr. Forster says we are not unemotional, but that our emotions come slowly and arrive late, and, like deep-sea fishes, find it difficult to rise to the surface; but English literature is a flying-fish, " a sample of the life that goes on day after day beneath the surface; it is a proof that beauty and emotion exist in the salt, inhospitable sea." This is a good conceit. Indeed, all the conceits, speculations and illustrations in this essay are good. But as a whole it is not good or original enough for Mr. Forster, who should perhaps leave it to less first-hand intelligences to make national generalizations and explain English hypocrisy. He seems, too, to have missed English mystical religion, that tremendous force in history, for he says:

" Is the Englishman altogether indifferent to the things of the spirit ? . . . Religion is more than an ethical code with a divine sanction. It is also a means through which man may get into direct connection with the divine, and, judging by history, few Englishmen have succeeded in doing this. We have produced no series of prophets. . . . We have not even produced a Joan of Arc or Savonarola. We have produced few saints. In Germany the Reformation was due to the passionate conviction of Luther. In England it was due to a palace intrigue. We can show a steady level of piety, a fixed determination to live decently according to our lights—little more."

Surely an odd judgment on a race which has produced Richard Rolle, Julian of Norwich, that vociferously lachrymose penitent, Margery Kempe, Wycliffe (as determined a Protestant Reformer as Luther), St. Thomas More, Tyndale, all the Protestant and Catholic martyrs, Lancelot Andrewes, John Donne, George Herbert, Crashaw, Vaughan, Traherne, William Law, all the God-intoxicated puritans and unruly, excited sectaries of the seventeenth century, dashing across the Atlantic with their cropped ears and branded cheeks to found a new world where unruly and excited sectaries should set the tone; the Quakers, communing closely with their God even at the stocks and whipping-post, John Wesley and the methodist enthusiasts, the nineteenth-century Tractarians and Evangelicals in tears over their sins and God's love. And had Mr. Forster remarked the curious and deplorable fact that English writers between the ninth and the fourteenth centuries, from Cædmon to Chaucer, spent the whole of their time, intelligence and parchment in writing theological treatises, religious histories of the world, long allegorical poems about God, the soul, and the deadly sins, a universal medieval Christian disease from which, however, the French and Germans recovered sufficiently to write love and adventure stories two and three centuries before the English ? Mr. Forster might reply that he was thinking only of the modern English: but even so, I should be inclined to guess that as much (there never is much anywhere) mystical religious feeling obtains among the English as among the French, Germans, Italians, Spanish or Dutch. We have certainly more queer sects than anyone but the Americans. However, such comparisons are fruitless: one cannot test them.

Mr. Forster anticipates a change in the English character in the next twenty years into " something that is less unique but more lovable. The supremacy of the middle classes is probably ending." The twenty years is nearly through: has such a change come ? Not yet, it seems; the middle classes and the public schools are still going strong, but their doom looks near. " What new element the working classes will introduce one cannot say, but at all events they will not have been educated at public schools." This public school business is rather perplexing. Can it really be that boys sent to live together for a few years to do lessons and play games, turn into something quite different from what they would have turned into if they had lived at home and attended day schools ? It is mysterious, but one must, I suppose, accept it, since they all say so. It sounds as if some out-side supernatural agent descended on boys gathered together and transformed them into a new creature: well, perhaps it does; but one would rather hear Mr. Forster explaining and analysing the process than assuming it.

On the whole, he is not at his happiest in the uncongenial company of this undeveloped middle-class Englishman, whom he never quite brings to life. Perhaps we have met him too often, or perhaps he bores his analyser, for whom he is, indeed, no fit companion; his company even affects and flattens Mr. Forster's style, and he very nearly becomes—incredible metamorphosis—a thoughtful and intelligent journalist.

One is glad when he turns instead to the so different, so delightful, so un-public-school, six-teenth-century Emperor Babur, whose *Memoirs* and vigorously predatory career he summarizes with the utmost sympathy.*

" The boy had inherited Ferghana, a scrubby domain at the extreme north of the fashionable world ; thinking Samarkand a suitable addition, he conquered it from an uncle when he was thirteen. . . . His affairs grew worse ; steal as he might, others stole quicker, and at eighteen his mother made him marry—a tedious episode. He thought of escaping to China,

* *Abinger Harvest.*

so hopeless was the block of uncles, and cousins, and aunts; poisoned coffee and the fire-pencil thinned them out, but only for a moment; up they sprang; again he conquered, lost, conquered and lost for ever Ferghana and Samarkand. Not until he was twenty-one, and had taken to drink, did the true direction of his destiny appear; moving southward, he annexed Kabul. . . . He took Delhi, he founded the Moghul Empire, and then, not to spoil the perfect outline of his life, he died. . . .

" These sanguine and successful conquerors generally have defects that would make them intolerable as companions. They are unobservant of all that does not assist them towards glory, and, consequently, vague and pompous about their past; they are so busy; when they have any charm, it is that of our Henry V—the schoolboy unpacking a hamper that doesn't belong to him. But what a happiness to have known Babur! He had all that one seeks in a friend."

Here again are all the familiar felicities of style; with this charming and plundering Asiatic Mr. Forster is at ease.

# CHAPTER XII

IN April, 1922, Mr. Forster wrote in his diary:
" Have read my Indian fragment, with a view to
continuing it." The Indian fragment had been
written after the 1912 visit; it expanded, through
1922 and 1923, into the novel *A Passage to India*,
which bears obvious marks of originating from
two different periods in the uneasy social history of
Indian and Anglo-Indian relationships. (One
doesn't, I know, call the English in India Anglo-
Indians in these days, as the name has been, rather
confusingly, transferred to Indians of mixed
descent, who used to be called Eurasians; having
lost that convenient and inoffensive word, I am
not sure what is the name for European and Indian
mixtures other than English. But Mr. Forster,
throughout his novel, uses Anglo-Indians in its
old and familiar sense, and I shall follow him.)

A good many things had happened to Indians
and to British India in the ten years between Mr.
Forster's two visits; the date of the novel is
apparently approximately that of the earlier visit.
Its place is Chandrapore, a town on the Ganges,
with a small British station. The first section of

the book is called "Mosque." Its first short
chapter describes Chandrapore; the second introduces Dr. Aziz, a young Mohammedan, calling on
two friends. They talk of the English; of how
the English have insulted them and continue perpetually to insult them. One of them, however,
mentions that some English, even some English
ladies, have shown him courtesy and kindness,
though mainly long ago when he was visiting
England—" I only contend that it is possible in
England. . . . They have no chance here. They
come out intending to be gentlemen, and are told
it will not do." Nevertheless, little kindnesses are
recalled: " but of course this is exceptional."
Then " the gleam passed from the conversation,
whose wintry surface unrolled and expanded in-
terminably. A servant announced dinner." They
dine. Aziz quotes poetry; the themes he prefers
are the decay of Islam and the brevity of love; the
others listen in delight. He is interrupted by a
note of summons from the Civil Surgeon, and
bicycles off in resentment to the Civil Surgeon's
bungalow, to find him already gone out. Vexed,
he walks away, and turns into a mosque to rest.
Here he meets and talks with Mrs. Moore, an
elderly Englishwoman newly come out to India to
visit her son, the young City Magistrate, who
insults Indians. But Mrs. Moore does not insult
Indians: she wants to know and understand them;
Aziz loves her for her sympathy.

M

Mrs. Moore returns from the mosque to the English club, and is plunged again among her countrymen and countrywomen. The girl Adela Quested, with whom she came out, who is probably to marry her son, says she wants to see " the real India." " Try seeing Indians," suggests a schoolmaster, the head of Government College. The ladies, amused at Miss Quested, cry " Wanting to see Indians! How new that sounds! " " Natives! Why, fancy," and " Let me explain. Natives don't respect one any the more after meeting one, you see." To which Adela, a sensible and accurate girl, returns " That occurs after so many meetings."

But the Collector says: " Do you really want to meet the Aryan Brother, Miss Quested ? That can be easily fixed up "—and offers to have " a Bridge Party," that is, a party to bridge the gulf between East and West.

Driving home, the Collector's wife criticizes Miss Quested, as queer and cranky and not pukka. Adela is not a success at the Station; no one but Ronny Heaslop likes her much, and he is critical, too. The Bridge Party is not a success, either. The Indians and the English are both uncomfortable. Two or three of the English officials make a few friendly remarks, but they are mostly preoccupied with the demands of their own womenfolk, and with tennis, in which the Indians do not join. Adela is ashamed and angry.

" Like a shutter, fell the vision of her married life. She and Ronny would look into the club like this every evening . . . while the true India slid by unnoticed. . . . She would see India always as a frieze, never as a spirit."

## Afterwards, Mrs. Moore talks to her son.

" 'Oh, look here,' he broke out, rather pathetically, 'what do you and Adela want me to do ? Go against my class, against all the people I respect and admire out here ? . . . It's morbidly sensitive to go on as Adela and you do. . . . I am out here to work, mind, to hold this wretched country by force. I'm not a missionary or a Labour Member or a vague sentimental sympathetic literary man. I'm just a servant of the Government. . . . We're not pleasant in India, and we don't intend to be pleasant. We've something more important to do.'

" He spoke sincerely. Every day he worked hard in the court trying to decide which of two untrue accounts was the less untrue, trying to dispense justice fearlessly, to protect the weak against the less weak. . . ."

## But his mother thinks that the English *are* out there to be pleasant.

" Because India is part of the earth. And God has put us on the earth to be pleasant to each other. . . . The desire to behave pleasantly satisfies God."

## Ronny thinks, " She is certainly ageing, and I ought not to be vexed with anything she says."

" Mrs. Moore felt that she had made a mistake in mentioning God, but she found him increasingly difficult to avoid as she grew older, and he had been constantly in her thought since she entered India, though oddly enough he satisfied her less. She must needs pronounce his name frequently, as the greatest she knew, yet she had never found it less efficacious.

Outside the arch there seemed always an arch, beyond the remotest echo a silence."

Later, Fielding, of the Government College, has Mrs. Moore and Miss Quested to tea, to meet Aziz and the Brahman Professor Godbole. Aziz, excited and above himself, invites the English ladies to a party of pleasure: he will conduct them to see the famous Marabar Caves. Into the tea-party bursts Ronny, all discourtesy, arrogance and impatience, and, ignoring the Indians, takes Adela and his mother away to watch polo.

Aziz and Fielding cultivate an experimental friendship: Aziz loves Fielding, Fielding is interested in Aziz, visits him when he is ill; they puzzle and surprise but please one another. The temperamental Aziz is happy: it is the last really happy hour that he has in the book.

Part II begins: it is called " Caves." Aziz invites Fielding and Professor Godbole to join his party to the Marabar Caves, an enterprise which, after his imprudent invitation, is forced upon him. But Fielding and Godbole miss the train, and he is left alone with the English ladies and some servants and a poor relation of his own. Dismayed at first, he rises to the great occasion. The train runs, the ladies are fed with poached eggs and tea every few minutes, Aziz having been warned that the English never stop eating; the train arrives and is met by an elephant, on whom they all ride through an unpleasing plain to the Caves.

All goes so well, so far, that Aziz is delighted.

"The expedition was a success, and it was Indian; an obscure young man had been allowed to show courtesy to visitors from another country, which is what all Indians long to do. . . . Hospitality had been achieved."

He loves Mrs. Moore increasingly: she is, he feels, his dear and honoured friend. He likes Miss Quested, though physically he is repelled by her. He feels and says, "One of the dreams of my life is accomplished in having you both here as my guests." They sit and converse about the Mogul Emperors, about brotherhood, about religion, about the Anglo-Indian problem. Miss Quested consults Aziz on this last; but he retreats into reserve and conducts them to the Caves.

The caves are not a success. In the first cave, Mrs. Moore nearly faints, from the crowd, the smell and the echo. She declines to visit the other caves, and Aziz and Adela proceed to them alone with a guide.

Then there is serious trouble: Adela, having entered a cave alone, feels something pull her about and tear off her field-glasses; she thinks it is Aziz, flies down the hill to an acquaintance who has just turned up in a car, and is driven home. Aziz thinks she has merely tired of the expedition. Fielding, who has arrived in the car, has walked up the hill and joins him and Mrs. Moore.

On the return of their train to Chandrapore, Aziz is arrested by the police and taken to prison.

Fielding, protesting, is informed that Aziz has insulted Miss Quested in a cave. He refuses to believe it; he sides with the Indians against the English. The English are roused to white-hot emotion by the incident; herd patriotism, herd anti-Indian anger shake them; they intoxicate themselves with the incantations of their caste. Only Fielding and Mrs. Moore hold aloof. Mrs. Moore, apparently suffering from a kind of sun-stroke, oppressed and haunted by the sinister echoes in the cave, has turned irritable and dis-agreeable and queer. Knowing Aziz to be inno-cent, she is surly to Adela. Adela is bewildered and confused: she is not sure what happened in the cave, or if anything did. Ronny Heaslop sends his mother home, to get her out of the way; she dies on the voyage through the Red Sea.

The trial of Aziz comes on. The affair has become a feud, English against Indians; feeling runs high. At the trial, Adela, whose head has been gradually clearing, suddenly realizes that Aziz is innocent, had not entered the cave at all, and withdraws the charge. There is pande-monium: rage among the English, shrieking triumph among the Indians. Everyone, except Ronny, broken-down and bewildered, and Field-ing, who is moved by the girl's honesty, insults Adela: she is excommunicated by the English for her recantation, execrated by the Indians for her accusation. Aziz is determined to exact huge

financial damages from her. Fielding tries to dis-
suade him from demanding money beyond his
costs. But he announces himself as having turned
completely anti-British, and will get all he can;
until at last Fielding uses the memory of Mrs.
Moore to persuade him to generosity, and, with a
noble gesture, he renounces his claim. Fielding
and he are now close friends. Adela, befriended
by Fielding only, talks over the situation with him,
decides that, on the whole, it may have been the
guide or some stranger who attacked her in the
cave, but that it matters little, and sails for England, thrown over by Ronny and all his com-
patriots.

At Chandrapore the Hindu-Moslem Indian
front against the English hardens. Suspicion and
gossip poison Aziz's friendship for Fielding; he
believes that his friend will marry Miss Quested
when he visits England, that she has already been
his mistress. Fielding's denials do not convince
him; his friends gossip him into deeper suspicion;
Chandrapore in the hot weather confirms his bad
fancies; he knows himself tricked and despoiled,
both of money and friendship. Fielding sails for
England, Aziz goes to work in an Indian state.
So, on failure and mistrust, ends this central
section of the book.

The last section is called " Temple." It is two
years later, and the scene is a Hindu festival in a
Temple at Mau, the festival of the birth of a God,

the birth of Shri Krishna, Infinite Love who saves the world. Professor Godbole leads a choir. There is singing and dancing and worship all night.

During the days of this festival, Fielding arrives at Mau; he is touring Central India, to investigate education. He is married: of course, thinks Aziz, to Miss Quested. Aziz has no wish to see him again. Aziz is working at Mau; he never sees English people, and Moslems seldom. He hates the English. He is happy enough, married again, writing poetry, riding. He is vexed by the arrival of Fielding and his wife. When he meets Fielding by accident, they coldly converse. Aziz learns that Fielding's wife is not Miss Quested, but the daughter of Mrs. Moore. Angry at his own mistake, he still sticks to its consequences; he says, " My heart is for my own people henceforward. I wish no Englishman or Englishwoman to be my friend."

But he and Fielding are later reconciled, and in the last chapter they go riding together in the jungle, " friends again, yet aware that they could meet no more." Aziz produces a letter he wants to send to Miss Quested, thanking her, at last, for her fine behaviour two years back. He says: " I want to do kind actions all round, and wipe out the wretched business of the Marabar for ever."

They talk: they agree that this is good-bye. Fielding too

" felt that this was their last free intercourse. All the stupid misunderstandings had been cleared up, but socially they had no meeting-place. He had thrown in his lot with Anglo-India by marrying a countrywoman, and he was acquiring some of its limitations."

Fielding talks of his wife and her brother, of the Hindu festival and Hindu religion; Aziz changes the subject to politics. They argue about the British in India. Aziz declares open war on them. Fielding defends them for their efficiency. He asks:

" ' Who do you want instead of the English ? The Japanese ? '

" ' No, the Afghans. My own ancestors.'

" ' Oh, your Hindu friends will like that, won't they ? '

" ' It will be arranged—a conference of Oriental statesmen.' "

Aziz, feeling himself in a corner, makes his horse rear and shouts, " India shall be a nation! No foreigners of any sort! Hindu and Moslem and Sikh and all shall be one! "

Fielding mocks him; Aziz cries,

" ' Down with the English anyhow. . . . We may hate one another, but we hate you most . . . if it's fifty five-hundred years we shall get rid of you, yes, we shall drive every blasted Englishman into the sea, and then . . . you and I shall be friends.'

" ' Why can't we be friends now ? ' said the other, holding him affectionately. ' It's what I want. It's what you want.'

" But the horses didn't want it—they swerved apart; the earth didn't want it, sending up rocks through which riders must pass single file ; the temples, the tank, the jail, the palace, the birds, the carrion, the Guest House, that came into view as they issued from the gap . . . they didn't want it, they said in their hundred voices, ' No, not yet,' and the sky said, ' No, not there.' "

So the book ends. English and Indians, remote as ever, are heading for open rupture; no individual friendships can stay this feud; even if individual friendship is possible. Will the new Indian Constitution stay it ? That is beyond the book's range; the new constitution is not yet in sight.

Those who demand precision want to know what is the novel's period.

" Until England is in difficulties," cries Aziz, " we keep silent, but in the next European war— aha, aha! Then is our time."

The European war is apparently still ahead. But the date does not matter very much. The social, psychological and racial problem is perpetual, it can be staged in any year, and the novel, anyhow, is not a newspaper record. It is taking it too much as this that has made some of the criticisms of *A Passage to India* irrelevant. Those who know India have emphasized that some details are wrong, that the setting of the trial is impossible, that the behaviour of the English is overdrawn. This last might, probably, be a matter of opinion; anyhow, opinions on it among the experienced differ. It is probable that Mr. Forster, shocked and startled by incivilities, arrogances and complacent obtusenesses observed by him, exaggerated them, spread them too widely. Still, there they are. Indians have *not* always been allowed to visit English clubs; English men and women *have* been heard to speak contemptuously of Indians; there *is* rudeness and insolence sometimes; rude women have been known to cut those they hold for inferiors, in all lands; a mixed garden party might well be a social failure; most of the incidents and speeches in the novel could be paralleled with facts. The emphasis is probably imperfect; it is difficult, in portraying a section of society, to get it perfectly right, and, though there are no doubt intolerable people like Major Callendar and Mrs. Turton, their prominence in the novel may give a wrong impression of their actual numbers. There are foolish and violent men and women everywhere; when Major Callendar, the Civil Surgeon, describes with tittering triumph his brutal treatment of a young Indian in hospital after a car smash, adding: " nothing's too bad for these people," and Mrs. Turton says: " they ought to crawl from here to the caves on their hands and knees whenever an Englishwoman's in sight, they oughtn't to be spoken to, they ought to be spat at, they ought to be ground into the dust," one remembers very similar speeches about our foes during the late European war, and that this, too, was a state of war, emotions, patriotism and racial phobia, for an English girl had been (so they supposed) insulted by an Indian. One cannot say that Callendars and Turtons and others would not have broken out thus; it is likely enough that they would. Would they also have cast out and boycotted the unfortunate young woman after her public retraction of her charge ? This is much more doubtful : it seems likely that some among them would have shown, if not more compassion, at least more decency, and would not have abandoned the girl to find shelter where she could. The solidity of English sahibs in a land of " natives " would probably have prevented this. Here, and occasionally elsewhere, it looks as if Mr. Forster's acutely vulnerable sense of humanity and his dislike of barbarous nationalism and uncivil arrogance had over-reached itself, and made him paint his natural enemies a shade too black.

This is the most serious charge that can be made against the novel, for it is a criticism of its psychology, its drawing of people; the other inaccuracies, in so far as they exist, are merely technical.

Some confusion is perhaps caused by the book's doubtful chronology, for it deals with the India of one period, is written largely from material collected and from a point of view derived from that period, and was published twelve years later, when Indians and English had got into quite another stage. In January, 1922, just after his second visit to India, Mr. Forster wrote two articles in the

*Nation and Athæneum*; he called them " Reflections in India," and one was subtitled " Too Late." It opens thus:

" Once upon a time an Indian whom I know undertook a railway journey in his own country. He had lain down to sleep when the door of the carriage opened and an Englishman entered and greeted him as follows : ' Here, get out of that.' The greeting was instinctive. The Englishman meant no harm by it. It was the sort of thing one had to say to a native whom one found sprawling in a first-class compartment, or what would happen to the British Raj ? . . .

" Ten years passed and the same man went for another railway journey. It was he who entered the carriage this time, while an Englishman, an officer, was in occupation. The latter sprang up with *empressement* and began to shift his kit. ' Here, take my berth, it's the best ; I'm getting out soon.' ' No, why should I ? ' ' Oh, no, take it, man, that's all right ; this is your country, not mine.' The Indian remarked grimly: ' Don't do this sort of thing, please. We don't appreciate it any more than the old sort. We know you have been told you must do it.' The unfortunate officer was silent. It was so. Orders had come down from Headquarters enjoining courtesy, and in his attempt to save the British Raj he had exceeded them.

" This hasty and ungraceful change of position is typical of Anglo-India to-day. Something like a stampede can be observed. Some officials have changed out of policy ; they know they can no longer trust their superiors to back them up if they are rude or overbearing. . . . Others have undergone a genuine change of heart. . . . They dread the reforms, but propose to work them. ' Yes, it's all up with us,' is their attitude. Sooner or later the Indians will tell us to go. I hope they'll tell us nicely. I expect they will—they're always very nice to me.'. . . The decent Anglo-Indian of to-day realizes that the great blunder of the past is neither political nor economic nor educational, but social; that he was associated with a system that supported rudeness in railway carriages, and is paying the penalty.

"The penalty is inevitable. The mischief has been done, and though friendships between individuals will continue and courtesies between high officials increase, there is little hope of spontaneous intercourse between the two races."

It is, in fact, too late. The damage is done. The Indian to-day has ceased to be sensitive to English snubs, he has become socially independent. Nationalism has swollen. The Englishwoman in India (worse than the Englishman) is, like her menfolk, quieter to-day.

"The lady who said to me eight years ago, 'Never forget that you are superior to every native in India except the Rajahs, and they're on an equality,' is now a silent, if not an extinct, species. But she has lived her life, and she has done her work."

So, though the state of things is now better, and there are now clubs where the two races can meet, it is still bad, and, though " responsible Englishmen are far politer to Indians than they were ten years ago, it is too late, because Indians no longer require their social support." " Never in history," the article sadly ends, " did ill-breeding contribute so much towards the dissolution of an Empire."

The sadness is not for the likely dissolution of the Empire, Empires being, in the writer's eyes, all the better for being dissolved, but for ill-breeding, the miserable tragedy of manners and of heart, which is largely the tragedy of this book, where rudeness spins the plot and the British Raj is betrayed by what is coarse within.

Granted, then, that the British sahibs and mem-sahibs are too gross for the India of the 1920's, and that the book would have been improved by being given a definite date, still how good they are in their lighter moments, how excellently caught their idiom! This delicate ear for idiom is one of Mr. Forster's gifts, which never seems to fail. Here, among this babel of voices (a much larger cast than in his other novels) one can tell, nearly every time, who is speaking; dislike for the type has not fused or confused the individual, though it does sometimes a little blur the edges.

But the major characters, both English and Indian, stand as solidly as any in the earlier novels. Adela, the charmless, honest, enquiring, sexless, slightly priggish young woman, drawn with nicety, balance, sympathy, and the most delicate exactitude, is a type belonging less to fiction than to life ; everything about her is true; unromantic realist, with no appeal beyond that of youth, integrity, and a civilized mind, she is a heroine rare in novels. She lacks the lively culture, wit and charm of the Schlegels, and the charming *ingénue* quality of Lucy Honeychurch; she is rather raw, a little like a modern Caroline Abbott, but more balanced and intelligent; and Caroline Abbott we never see from within, for at that time her creator was awkward and external with his female characters. In *A Passage to India*, there are two female principals, young Miss Quested and old Mrs. Moore. Mrs. Moore is another of Mr. Forster's superb elderly ladies; like Mrs. Wilcox, she has mystic apprehensions, she knows things by what Adela awkwardly calls " telepathy "; but she is intelligent, where Mrs. Wilcox is stupid; she has an educated sort of mind; like Adela, she is enquiring, and wants to know " the real India." Young Dr. Aziz loves her from their first meeting, and she is drawn toward him. She knows him to be innocent of the charge against him; but the caves have upset, almost deranged her, she is ill and out of humour, and can and will make no effort to clear him. Her mood through this affair is not explained; with Adela, whom she could have convinced with a word, and so prevented the trial, we are left outside her mind, baffled and guessing. All we see is that she feels un-well, that she is vexed and hostile with Adela and Ronny and anxious to get back to England. She will not speak up for poor Aziz, she has turned definitely queer, and will only play patience and snub the young people. Her behaviour has the awkward, uncompromising unexpectedness of actuality; it fits in with nothing we look for, it accommodates no preconceived notions or con-ventions, it is out of real life, and does not help the book out in the least. We never even learn whether, as Adela later thought, she knew, or

thought she knew, what had happened in the cave.
She sails for England without a word; and Aziz,
had he known Patmore, would have thought it all
unlike her great and gracious ways to go her
journey of all days with huddled, unintelligible
phrase and no word for him.  To be sure, the
thought of her, perhaps even, it is hinted, the
return of her spirit in the hour of her death, comes
to clarify Adela's confused mind in court and convince her of her mistake;  to be sure her name is
chanted by the Indians outside the court room,
like that of a goddess, and sacred shrines are built
for her; but that is after her death.  Before death,
she remains enigmatic, baffled and baffling;  the
caves and their sinister echoes annihilate in her
faith, hope and love;  her spirit is beaten down,
she becomes a surly defeatist, "sunk in apathy
and cynicism," only fit to play patience and to go
home in the heat, and not actually fit, as it proved,
for that.  She must have been, one sees, enchanting
in earlier life, full of that eager response to all
experience and that curiosity about the world
which marks all Mr. Forster's likeable characters.
The Marabar caves, which ruin every one, into
which obviously no one should ever go, which
land Aziz in prison, Adela in disgrace, Ronny in
loneliness and bereavement, Fielding in em-
barrassments, the English colony in baulked rage,
the guide (if it was the guide) in assault, ruin Mrs.
Moore's health, temper and soul.  She hates them

N

from the first, seeing them at once for what they are, and, very sensibly, liking no caves, whereas the others, more obtuse, do not object to them until afterwards. They brood over the book, disagreeable and sinister, with an odd, unexplained power.

Aziz is insensitive to caves; he only understands things and people when his affections are moved. He is a brilliantly drawn figure, more living than any of the Englishmen; an extraordinary tour-de-force in the portraiture of one race by another. Restless, friendly, volatile, vain, he darts emotionally about, like an affectionate and self-conscious peacock, happy in talking with his friends, resentfully sensitive to English snubs, fixing his affections on any new friend who will sympathize with him, pouring out his heart, his grievances, his affairs, passionately racially patriotic, lavishly hospitable, generous to his friends and his guests, vulgarly insulting when angry, often a bounder, shocking Fielding by his common and unchivalrous taunts, pleasing him by his confidences.

" Can't you see that fellow's a bounder ? " Ronny says to Fielding. Aziz, uneasily flamboyant, is patronizing Mrs. Moore. " He isn't a bounder," Fielding protests. " His nerves are on edge, that's all."

But a bounder Aziz often is. He is also a poet, a romantic liar, a poser, a loyal friend, a loving parent, a devoted widower, and a furious enemy. Full of vivacity, charm, and spiritual eagerness, he pleases Mrs. Moore, Adela and Fielding, and gets on the nerves of those English who think that natives should keep their places. He resents the English because they despise him; he despises Hindus (except old Professor Godbole) because they are Hindus, and make him think of cow-dung. Among his friends, he is all animation. The opening conversation of the book, between Aziz, Hamidullah, and Mahmoud Ali, has an air of the most convincing authenticity. This writing by an Englishman about a social gathering of three Mohammedan Indians is a feat which must, if we remember other such gatherings described by other English writers, dazzle us by its sheer virtuosity. So also must a later gathering, when four Mohammedans, two Hindus, and an Englishman assemble and gossip with spite and animation round Aziz's sick-bed. Both are extremely witty conversation pieces, brilliantly executed. In the first, Aziz is seen to be a gay and endearing creature; his two friends are intelligent, cultured, and embittered; all three, voicing Indian resentment about English discourtesy, are moving. Aziz, as we first met him, a receptive bundle of quick impressions, may, we feel, become anything, take any turn; a mutable man, the treatment he receives will mould him. The English are rude and inconsiderate to him: he is anti-English. He turns into a mosque to rest, and tries to

> " symbolize the whole into some truth of religion or love. A mosque, by winning his approval, let loose his imagination. The temple of another creed, Hindu, Christian, or Greek, would have bored him and failed to awaken his sense of beauty. Here was Islam, his own country, more than a faith, more than a battle-cry, more, much more. . . . Islam, an attitude towards life both exquisite and durable, where his body and his thoughts found their home."

In it he becomes a mystic, a poet, tuned to all fine issues.

Meeting, a moment later, Mrs. Moore, who talks to him with courteous friendliness, he becomes gentle, grateful, happy. Grievances do not matter any more. He is not, indeed, allowed to enter the English club, but

> " as he strolled down-hill beneath the lovely moon, and again saw the lovely mosque, he seemed to own the land as much as anyone owned it. What did it matter if a few flabby Hindus had preceded him there, and a few chilly English succeeded ? "

Practising polo with a friendly subaltern, he feels cheerful and free, forgetting race antagonisms in sport; invited to tea by Fielding, the Principal of Government College, he is elated and affectionate. Arriving there, he is overcome by warm and generous feelings, by affection for his host; he chatters at ease to Fielding and the two sympathetic English ladies; wild hospitality dizzies him, and he invites the ladies to an expedition with him; he is happy, excited, at ease.

Heaslop enters, treats him rudely; he becomes aggressive, flamboyant, provocative, showing off. Fielding visits him during a slight illness; they exchange confidences, Aziz feels he has made a friend, peace and happiness return to his soul, the world harmoniously blooms. On the expedition to the caves he rises to his top note; he is generous, hospitable, happy, triumphant, the successful host of English ladies, his friends. There follows the unjust charge, disgrace, trial, vindication: from then on he is savagely embittered, vowing revenge, resolved to exact the last farthing of redress from his false accusers; yet suddenly, pressed by Fielding, and by his memory of Mrs. Moore, he yields, and renounces all compensation. Enraged against the English, he is driven towards a Moslem-Hindu entente; he is now anti-English for ever, he loves India as his motherland, despite her contending races, and vows to see more of non-Mohammedan Indians. Shaking the dust of British India off his feet, he goes to work in an Indian state. On the flimsiest of reasons, he decides that Fielding will marry his enemy Miss Quested. He escapes from the English, who have frightened him permanently. Two years later he and Fielding meet again; they mend their broken friendship, but Aziz remains anti-English, crying " India shall be a nation! No foreigners of any sort! Hindu and Moslem and Sikh and all shall be one! "

Yet such is his mutability that if, after the book's end, he should mix with friendly English, or become disgusted with Hindus, we feel that he may drop this cry. He is like that; blown about on changing gusts of emotion, a sanguine, mercurial man.

This portrait alone would make *A Passage to India* a great novel. Foiled by the bluff, placid Englishman Fielding, by the serene, sly old Hindu Professor Godbole, by the complacent group of English officials, he alone touches our hearts, the others are approved by our intelligence. He is the spirit of young, forward, Moslem India, callow, aggressive, sensitive, nursing his hurts, fonding loyally on his friends, rallying them in the most horrible of outworn English slang. He has been said by fellow-countrymen to be an admirable portrait.

The question puts itself, what kind of novel is *A Passage to India*? A good story? Yes; for Mr. Forster is a good story-teller; at plot-contrivance he is an adept. The novel, as he has regretfully said himself, must tell a story; one supposes this to be true; anyhow, it had better; and anyhow his novels always do. *A Passage to India* is, in fact, a remarkably well-built tale, with significant approach, tense suspense, highly dramatic crisis, brilliantly narrated *dénouement*, and fine close. A good story, then, by all means, as were all the earlier novels.

Next, what is its main preoccupation? What is it getting at? The great human battle again, the war between integrity and humbug, reality and sham? No, that moral contest scarcely lifts a lance here; the banners are different. Personal relationships, then? Not very much; they are vivid, but not dominant. Mrs. Moore "felt increasingly (vision or nightmare?) that, though people are important, the relations between them are not." The emphasis has shifted. Aziz declares in the end that he and Fielding can never be friends until the English have been driven from India. Race has sucked each of the friends into his own background, they stand in opposed camps, affectionate enemies; the personal relationship, which in *Howards End* is to be the general solvent, is here less inadequate than irrelevant, beside the mark. There are too many Indians, too many English, for such a solution. Kindness, indeed, remains an essential—" I assure you it is the only hope," says Aziz. "We can't build up India except on what we feel."

But kindness is not enough to bridge the great race gulf. Even were all the English in India like Mrs. Moore and Fielding, it would not be bridged, it is too wide. Each race is to the other " people whose emotions they could not share." They offend one another. Aziz mocks plain Adela to Fielding, and promises to provide him with " a lady with breasts like mangoes"; Adela asks

Aziz, meaning no harm, how many wives he has, and he thinks, " Damn the English even at their best." When Aziz and Fielding argue, " something racial intruded—not bitterly, but inevitably, like the colour of their skins." Misunderstandings interrupt their intercourse—" a pause in the wrong place, an intonation misunderstood, and a whole conversation went awry." It is a case of mass misunderstanding, of different - complexioned, different-speaking, different-minded peoples staring at one another myopically across a ravine. Great races with different heritage and history, neither desiring to understand the other, and one of them in the wrong place.

Such is the enlargement of the " personal relations " that was a main theme of *Howards End*. The idea, thus extended, is applied to a particular social and political problem. The average English official in India is represented by Mr. Forster as rude, stupid, and unkind in his relations with " the Aryan brother," he is almost a Gerald Dawes, a Charles Wilcox, a Mr. Eager, his memsahib (worse) a Harriet Herriton. But, whatever they might be, he seems to say, it would not do. And that, I suppose, is the main theme of *A Passage to India*.

The publication of a novel after a gap of fourteen years since the author's last makes more than usually interesting the examination of the development of the way he writes. Comparing *A Passage*

*to India* with the earlier novels, one notices differences. There is greater seriousness and depth,
even sadness, more poetry, more beauty, less wit.
India broods over the scene with an extraordinary
effect of mysterious and sinister power. Everything Indian is haloed in mystery; the caves, the
landscape, even the bird that the English see in a
tree and cannot identify, for " nothing in India is
identifiable, the mere asking of a question causes it
to disappear and to merge in something else." An
animal dashes into a car in the dusk; no one can
identify that either; it is a goat, a hyena, the ghost
of a slain man. A girl believes herself attacked in
a cave; she is and she is not; her assailant is her
imagination, the guide, a villager, a Pathan; since
it is India, no one knows, and we shall never know;
Sherlock Holmes himself would, had he been
summoned, have had to record the case as one of
his failures. The mosque of Islam is mysterious,
and the festival of the Hindu temple; Mrs.
Moore, in England no doubt just a nice and intelligent elderly lady, becomes in India a mystic,
almost a goddess, superhumanly attributed,
apprehensive, and in the end inapprehensible, the
Esmiss Esmoor of a chanting crowd. All the
vague, hinted mysticism of the earlier novels, and
the cruder supernaturalisms of the short stories,
find fulfilment here, transcended in a deep, brooding mysticness, in which ugliness and beauty merge.

In conveying a scene, whether of mystery,

beauty, or sinister fear, Mr. Forster has advanced in this book to new powers. The city of Chandrapore, the flat, light-drowned earth beneath the huge vault of sky and sun, the mosque in moonlight, Dr. Godbole singing unintelligibly to Shri Krishna at an English tea-party, the hills, the caves, the train journey to these in the dawn, the elephant ride through a colourless granite land, the magnificently done Krishna festival at Mau— these demand and call forth powers of description, of direct, vivid transmission of odd and beautiful scenes, at which passages in the earlier books only hint. The poet, always a prominent partner in his work, here has scope and rein. *A Passage to India* will live as a social-political tract, flawed in many eyes by supposed bias and even inaccuracies; as a psychological novel, damaged here and there in some eyes by over-mystification and queerness; as a superb character study of people of one race by a writer of another; as an absorbing story, marred by some improbabilities; but most, I think, for its sheer beauty. The words, the precise, unpurpled, clear detail, as unexpected, as un-literary, as if one were seeing a new scene for one-self, has the qualities of the kind of verse, or the kind of painting, which derives straight from the poet's or the artist's vision, recorded simply because it is seen to be there, not rounded off to make a conventional picture, or neatly arranged like a surrealist's dream.

As to its moral—(has it one ? Of course: Mr. Forster always has, and is one of the few English novelists who can, by pointing a moral, adorn a tale)—it may perhaps be summed up in a paragraph that he wrote in a review (1925) of a translation of Anatole France's *Joan of Arc*.

" But the legions of ought and ought not will never assist us, any more than they assisted the rival assemblies of Poitiers and Rouen. Back reels the world into darkness, and amid cries of ' Devil—no, I mean Angel,' the empty processes of condemnation and rehabilitation are repeated. When will the day dawn ? When shall we be weary of passing moral or medical judgments, and attempt instead to understand ? "

# CHAPTER XIII

## IRONIES AND APPRECIATIONS

THE success of *A Passage to India* was immense. Through the last dozen years, Mr. Forster's stock had quietly rolled up; he was regarded, after *Howards End*, as a major novelist; his reputation towered—spired is better—up into those literary heights where the reputations of authors are enskied, beyond the few and beyond cliques. Whether *A Passage to India* was a " best-seller " or not, I do not know, nor what this curious expression implies: " best " should mean, one would suppose, better than any other. (Does one, by the way, speak of " best-singers," or " best-writers," or " best-painters " ? Very likely one does.) But how many copies of a book must sell to sell " best " ? Some reply, ten thousand; others, more soaring, twenty thousand, or fifty; there are, they say, who stipulate for figures still more astronomical. It is enough to record here that *A Passage to India* sold a large number of copies, not only in these islands, but in America.

As regards this latter land, Mr. Forster remarked, in an article called " My Wood,"* written in 1926:　　　　* *Abinger Harvest.*

" Feeling that they would have had no difficulties in India themselves, the Americans read the book freely. The more they read it the better it made them feel, and a cheque to the author was the result. I bought a wood with the cheque. It is not a large wood. . . ."

Not large, but it furnished the occasion for a very pretty essay on the psychological effects of property on its owners. It makes them feel heavy, it produces men of weight, who cannot easily slip into the Kingdom of Heaven. Then, too, it makes them feel that the property ought to be larger, it should be rounded off with the vineyards of other owners, beyond it, it should be extended without limit. Thirdly, the property owner is for ever wanting to do something to it, to remove or add trees, to express himself. Finally, he wants to keep other people out, to build walls about the footpath, to fence off his blackberries and foxgloves for his own use.

This ironic essay has, I think, some significance in its writer's development; it was written in a period when the unfair inequalities and social and economic cruelties of human life were pressing on his attention more inescapably than before. There was India and its racial problems, snarled almost past disentangling in the bitter traditions of mistrust; there was the nearer East, which still held hope (for this, and much else, read the pamphlet *Notes on Egypt*, and the article *Salute to the Orient* (1923)*; there were the poor, the

* *Abinger Harvest.*

oppressed, the freaks, the out of step, the queer, all those straying, straggling, struggling errants of the various underworlds, sympathy with whom should be nicely measured and balanced if it is to be right, for if poured forth to excess it becomes unbalanced, in fact, left. Left, in this sense, Mr. Forster's mind had always been; it showed signs in the post-war years of becoming still more so.

Left, left, left: the march of a great miscellaneous army goes to that beat, and of it some marchers are generously, some selfishly angry; some are compassionate; some hate wealth, others want it; some desire democracy, others a proletarian rule; some have a passion for liberty, others for compulsion; all are against the rule of the rich and things as they are. From every point of view Mr. Forster is bound to be left; he dislikes oppressors and empires and top dogs, the rich, the sleek, the heavy; his sympathies are with the people underneath, behind and outside the right places and the right clubs. Were he a Russian, he would have been against the Czars and would have revolted with Kerensky, have gone Red, and would now, presumably, be White in sympathies so long as Whites are oppressed. Being English, he is anti-imperialist, anti-capitalist, pro-poor, and always pro-rebel and pro-oddity. He prefers the eccentric, those, that is, who are outside the briskly spinning wheel that carries most of us round.

In 1925 he wrote an article about the exhibition of Sargent portraits at the Royal Academy, called " Me, Them and You."*

" Them what ?  Them persons what governs us, them dukes and duchesses and archbishops and generals and captains of industry."

Mr. Forster does not care for Them; he gently mocks Them, he is, no doubt, unfair to some of Them: how, for example, does he know that the voice which would proceed from the wife of our then Ambassador at Berlin, " superbly beautiful and incredibly arrogant," though she looked, besides hung with pearls, would not be a voice to promote amity between nations, or that her theme would necessarily be precedence ?  He does not know, but he feels sure, for he does not like the lady.

Nor the rest of Our Betters.

" Gazing at each other over our heads, they said, What would the country do without us ?  We have got the decorations and the pearls, we make fashions and wars, we have the largest houses and the best food, and control the most important industries, and breed the most valuable children, and ours is the Kingdom and the Power and the Glory. And, listening to their chorus, I felt that this was so, and my clothes fitted worse and worse, and there seemed in all the universe no gulf wider than the gulf between Them and Me—no wider gulf, until I encountered You.

" You had been plentiful enough in the snow outside (your proper place) but I had not expected to find you here in the place of honour, too. Yours was by far the largest picture in

* *Abinger Harvest.*

the show. You were hung between Lady Cowdray and the Hon. Mrs. Langham, and You were entitled ' Gassed.' You were of godlike beauty—for the upper classes only allow the lower classes to appear in art on condition that they wash themselves and have classical features. These conditions you fulfilled. A line of golden-haired Apollos moved along a duck-board from left to right with bandages over their eyes. They had been blinded by mustard gas. Others sat peacefully in the foreground. . . . The battlefield was sad but tidy . . . no one looked lousy or over-tired . . . and Lady Cowdray and the Hon. Mrs. Langham, as they looked over the twenty feet of canvas that divided them, were still able to say, ' How touching,' instead of ' How obscene.'

" Still, there you were, though in modified form, and in mockery of your real misery, and though the gulf between Them and Me was wide, still wider yawned the gulf between us and You. For what could we do without you ? What would become of our incomes and activities if you declined to exist ? You are the slush and dirt on which our civilization rests, which it treads under foot daily, which it sentimentalizes over now and then, in hours of danger. But you are not only a few selected youth in khaki, you are old men and women and dirty babies also. . . . ' For in Thee also a godlike frame lay hidden, but it was not to be unfolded,' not while the hard, self-satisfied faces stare at each other from the walls and say, ' But at all events we founded the Charity Organization Society—and look what we pay in wages, and look what our clothes cost, and clothes mean work.'

" The misery goes on, the feeble impulses of good return to the sender, and far away, in some other category, far away from the snobbery and glitter in which our souls and bodies have been entangled, is forged the instrument of the new dawn."

From much the same angle, but in more sardonic mood, and in verse, he had, two years before,

derided Bishop Welldon's complaint of the
" vulgar profanity " of the language used by
Labour Members of Parliament:

> " I have always been used to the best of things,
> I was nourished at Eton and crowned at King's,
> I pushed to the front in religion and play,
> I shoved all competitors out of the way ;
> I ruled at Harrow, I went to Calcutta,
> I buttered my bread and jammed my butter,
> And returned as a bishop, enormous of port,
> Who stood in a pulpit and said what he thought.
> Yes, I said what I thought and thought what I said,
> They hadn't got butter, they hadn't got bread,
> They hadn't got jam or tobacco or tea,
> They hadn't a friend, but they always had me.
> I can bully or patronize, just which I please ;
> I am different to them. . . . But those Labour M.P.s,
> How *dare* they be rude ? They ought to have waited
> Until they were properly educated. . . ."*

And so on. Good enough and sharp enough;
too sharp, indeed, for the delicately modulated
irony that would have informed it in prose, for
verse is too brisk and downright to be Mr.
Forster's proper medium; this piece of satire
and the other, *The Voter's Dilemma*,* of the same
year, about the liberal and conservative candidates
who stand for the same things, are not recognizable
Forster, they might be by any sharp and pointed
verse satirist; they say what is required, and say
it well, but without the adorning graces we are
used to :

* *Abinger Harvest.*

O

" And thus, whichever way I vote,
I get into the same old boat,
And Mr. Brown and Mr. Grey
Are rowing it the same old way—
The way of blood and fire and tears
And pestilence and profiteers—
The way that all mankind has been
Since nineteen hundred and fourteen.
Nice Mr. Grey ! Nice Mr. Brown !
Why trouble to come down from town ? "

It does well enough, and is bitter and sardonic enough. But had it been prose one would have smiled more and been sadder and angrier about politicians, yet more tolerant of nice Messrs. Grey and Brown. With verse, Mr. Forster can convey conviction, irony, anger, but not the shifting modulations of light and shade that move like flickering airs through the cadences of his prose, and which turn even dislike to a kind of friendly and amused understanding.

In such a manner he describes the British Empire Exhibition at Wembley in 1924,* which he inspected before it officially opened and enjoyed very much; and I have read no account of that Exhibition, or of any other Empire Exhibition, which has made it sound at once so endearing and so silly. This is the right way to make fun of empires and of Empire Exhibitions, and of Royal Dolls' Houses. Under such smiling mockery, empire itself becomes a dolls' house, an

* *Abinger Harvest.*

amusing toy, harmless and comic, like the Prince of Wales in butter.

Empires can be thus lightly bantered, even from the left. Not so Tyranny. When Liberty, that mountain nymph for ever in jeopardy, threats to whose all too violable chastity so excite and perturb our spirits, is assaulted, Mr. Forster takes a grave view of the matter. Liberty, since the horrible war which nearly disintegrated her altogether, has led an increasingly perilous life. Freedom of utterance on the part of the B.B.C. is assailed; rumours fly about of official tyranny, of interference from government departments and foreign embassies; it is past a joke. Human liberty; civil liberties; intellectual liberty; free culture; the battle for these, against the sinister enemies who would encroach on them, does not rest, and incessantly the artist must leave his ivory tower, or his flat, or his country cottage, or whatever it is he lives in, and take up arms to defend his heritage. Tyranny is like war, to be passionately hated; one cannot be on jesting terms with either.

But it was not till the 1930's that liberty, being more and more threatened in more and more places, became, though always distraught, really distracting to English writers. Through the 1920's—(a decade now much slandered, for people have begun inventing labels for it, as they have loved to do for all periods, and it has been tagged as fast and loose and wild and even "dirty")—through, then, the 1920's, which he found none of these things, Mr. Forster was largely occupied with comments on literature. He was doing a certain amount of reviewing of new books; some were good books, others less good; to both he brings a felicity of judgment and of phrase that is not satire, scarcely even irony; so light is the touch, so tolerant the smile, so enhancing of whatever qualities, good and bad, exist; and the odd result is achieved that, even when perceiving the book to be foolish and absurd, we conceive also a liking for its writer, and get the impression that the reviewer also likes him; it is like being introduced at a party to someone by a friend, who says: " Here is so-and-so, he's a nice, silly chap, but I see what he means, don't let's hurt his feelings more than we need." A pretty fusion of humanity, intellectuality, tolerance and humour does it, and the worst nonsense becomes nonsense of which we rather like to hear.

The æsthetic judgments are subjective rather than institutional and referred; they have the immediacy of personal taste; they derive from criteria which are implicit rather than stated; they emerge in flashes, like darting birds; yet they are a background, from which even the lightest comments come, a background steady, if unobtruded. Interest is mainly concentrated on the work under examination, often so entertaining as to distract from critical theory and lead along cheerful paths through decorated foregrounds, where we pluck the flowers and investigate the animals through enhancing bird-glasses, feeling that they are enough in themselves without comparing them with what they ought to be; definitely the English method not the French. Zest and penetration go hand in hand, and wit flatters the reader into borrowed discernment; even, perhaps, flatters the reviewed author into sharing the fun.

Did Mr. C. M. Doughty share the fun when his book *Mansoul* was reviewed ? *Mansoul* was not admired, nor (greatly) Mr. Doughty as a writer: here is the description of this infernal expedition:

" The old hackneyed business of a visit to the under-world —so tiring, such a getting downstairs, so dark, magic mirror, etc. . . . The conversation is such as is used on infernal occasions . . . Zoroaster, Confucius, Buddha, Socrates, and the other heavies each utter appropriate redes . . . Mansoul learns, as the result of his wanderings, that Faith, Love, Patriotism, etc., are English virtues, and that uneath, ment, derne, scruzed, tyned, stover, totty and blebs are English words."

Obvious nonsense, we conclude that *Mansoul* is: but nonsense, Mr. Forster implies, on the grand and respectable scale, and written by a grand and remarkable old gentleman, who, while one criticises,

" seems to lift his leonine head, and to intimate that if he thought it worth while he could stop his booming, and could explain why he was crabbed in his diction and obvious in his thoughts, why he constructed sentences upside down and punctuated them inside out, why he quotes from Homer neither in English nor in Greek, but in Italian. . . . Judged by standards other than literary, he ranks very high "—

being sincere, independent, dignified, and fearing no man. And so we like and admire Doughty, though we shall not read *Mansoul*.

Sifting and weighing proceeds, unimposed on either by fame, the merits of the good, or the imposingly Central European names of the bad, names as eccentrically Slav and remote from British conventions as Przbyszewski and Vrchlicky, which often hypnotize English critics as snakes rabbits, inducing a pop-eyed suspension of faculties.

" Przbyszewski is a Pole who writes about Chopin. He seems awfully bad—sentimental, Chauvinistic, grandiose. Ducic doesn't seem good either—a Serbian poet, influenced by Parisian cliques. . . . The note most frequently struck in the anthology is the patriotic, and—as in England and elsewhere—it is frequently struck on an inferior instrument. There is too much of ' O my country ! Ha the foeman ! ' with the names of country and foeman inserted according to geographical requirements. The foeman is usually Teuton— but he may be Armenian, or Latin, or Greek, and after a little one wearies of the formula, and remembers that a patriot cannot produce literature out of his patriotism any more than a lover can produce it out of his love : there must be something else in either case—some distinction of spirit that existed before the passion has stirred and remains after it has sunk— something greater than a nation, greater than personal joy and pain, something that lies beneath the superficialities of incident and can appeal to men who are not Slavs, who have not suffered. Such a quality seems to lurk in the queer verses of Beyruc, a Czech. . . .

"The Serbs seem less authentic : they give one the impression of turning out a literature in a hurry in order to qualify for the Comity of Nations. The Bulgarians are omitted from this anthology, no doubt for political reasons. . . ."

In the anthology there is one poem beautiful, poignant and great, it is Polish, and about a king and a peasant who both went to the wars: the king returned, with pealing bells of victory, the peasant stayed, buried in a pit in a wood.

"Such a poem rings truer than ' O my country ! Ha ! the foeman ! ' It is greater than nationalism, and greater than internationalism also. It has reached the land beyond either, where literature alone can have her being, and whither every writer, whatever his local passions, must aspire."

This poet, a female Pole, is unknown to British fame. Conversely, such heavy-weights as Dostoevsky can be sifted and criticized this side idolatry: yes, and even *Ulysses*. Here is a note on some Dostoevsky stories:

"Some are so feeble that they should dispel the superstition that Dostoevsky can do no wrong. It is a dangerous superstition, because only the more intelligent people hold it. The great Russian . . . is too often held up like a knout before the new generation of English novelists, with the result that they flagellate themselves with him unskilfully, and mistake the weals that he has raised upon their style for literature. Abruptness, obscurity, sudden tracts of gibber-gee and tvoo—such is the legacy the master will leave English fiction, unless we are careful. As a stimulus he is invaluable, as a model he may be disastrous. He has penetrated—more deeply, perhaps, than any English writer—into the darkness and the goodness of the human soul but he has penetrated by a way we cannot follow. He has his own psychological method. . . . But it is not ours. And like all methods it sometimes breaks down, and it is salutary to note the failure in most of the stories under review."

And here is *Ulysses*:

" It is in every sense a formidable work. Even the police are said not to comprehend it fully. . . . Pages that contain no nouns, or no verbs, or no stops, or nothing but newspaper headlines. . . . And the citizen who does survive the ordeal and gets to the end is naturally filled with admiration at his own achievement, and is apt to say that here is a great book, the book of the age. He really means that he himself is a great reader.

" The book of the age ? The book that will sum up our civilization as the Divine Comedy summed up Medievalism ? No one yet knows which book that is, or whether it can be written, but assuredly *Ulysses* is not that book. . . .

" Joyce is horrified and fascinated by the human body ; it seems to him ritually unclean and in direct contact with all the evil in the universe, and though to some of us this seems awful tosh, it certainly helps him to get some remarkable literary effects. . . ."

His complaint against *Ulysses* is that, aiming at holding up a mirror to our age (actually was it not to a particular day in Dublin some thirty years ago ?) it is a faulty mirror, reflecting only the mud and lusts, the false teeth sagging in the mouth, and all that. There are, Mr. Forster would protest, those with real teeth, or with false teeth that fit, there is beauty and fineness. Joyce, he says, is angry and peevish, he snarls, and tries to spatter the universe with mud, much of which does not stick but bounces back.

In point of fact, Mr. Forster dislikes mud and mess and snarling (he does not, I believe, keep a dog); and "tosh" about the uncleanness of the body bores both his fastidiousness and his sense of humour. He could admire Joyce's power, but be impatient with his manners and his attitude.

Crossness and bad manners and ungeniality bother him. He has a perplexed try at the enigmatic and divided Dean Inge,

> " He is an extraordinary fellow. He is so sensitive, so truth-seeking, so noble-minded, so realistic and brave, so reticent and sincere in his mysticism, that often he seems a really great interpreter who will lead us through the tangle of modern life as Virgil led Dante through medievalism. And then—woe is me !—he catches sight of his lodestar. ' There is the Labour Party,' he bawls. ' We see clear at last. It has as its main aim the unhappiness of the human race.' And I start, like one who awakes from a dream, and I find that I am holding by the hand, not Virgil, but a perverse, bumptious, and ill-tempered child, who shall answer to the name of Tommy. What are we to do with Tommy ? I do not like to smack him, because just a minute ago he was being intelligent and nice. Yet I can scarcely accept him as my guide."

The flaw in the analogy is that Virgil (Dante's Virgil, that is) could be on occasion perverse, bumptious and ill-tempered himself, and was quite capable of making similar outrageous remarks about the suffering souls.

" In his works of scholarship," Mr. Forster adds . . .
" Dean Inge's divided personality does not appear. But it
crops up as soon as he approaches the heat of social problems,
and it makes him difficult to follow. . . . I can't get to grips
with such a book."

With Ibsen,* also a divided personality, also
irritable, a nagger, he gets to grips better, and
makes of him a poet, a primeval submarine
figure, deep-sea-rooted and bewitched.

" For this nagging quality, this habitual bitterness—they are
essential in his greatness, because they beckon to the poetry in
him, and carry it with them under the ground. Underground.
Into the depths of the sea, the depths of the sea. Had he been
of heroic build and turned to the light and the sun, his gifts
would have evaporated. But he was—thank heaven—sub-
terranean, he loved narrow passages and darkness. . . . To
his impassioned vision dead and damaged things, however
contemptible socially, dwell for ever in the land of romance,
and this is the secret of his so-called symbolism. . . . Ibsen
is at bottom Peer Gynt. Side whiskers and all, he is a boy
bewitched."

The whole essay is a piece of brilliant analytic
construction.

The criticisms of contemporary literature now
interpret, now assess, now examine; throughout
the note is of critical integrity, the achievement is
imaginative interpretation, even when, as with
T. S. Eliot,* the punctuation is largely marks of
interrogation. Good, witty and profound comments grow in all these essays as thickly as

* *Abinger Harvest.*

blackberries in a bramble patch; only occasionally there is one which would appear not well found, as that Ronald Firbank's novels,* being "fundamentally unserious," disconcert the Anglo-Saxon reader, "who approves of playfulness, but likes it to have a holiday air." This, of a race which has flocked in idolatry after so many urbane and unriotous wits—Lamb, Oscar Wilde, Max Beerbohm, Norman Douglas, Logan Pearsall Smith, and other elegant ironists—seems inapt, and as if taken over from some less fastidious mind. For Mr. Forster's habit is to arrive at his own facts, rejecting facile generalizations; his words follow one another like sincere, fastidious explorers, seeking and finding truth, now darting, now hesitant, never tripping in glib sequence towards a goal at which it is proper to arrive. One would rather that this tired, much nagged-at creature, the Anglo-Saxon reader, were given a new, a less worn and familiar face, he is out of step with his fellows in these essays, in which nearly everything is a new creature; in most people's books we should say, either with resignation or irritation, "Of course, just the man we expected to see." It is the faculty for supplying the idea and the word that we do not expect to see, and that, when we see it, we perceive to be true, that gives these appreciations and criticisms their organic character.

* *Abinger Harvest.*

But it is, I think, when the person discussed is remote enough, in period or distance, or merely in accidental lack of contact, to emerge in the round as a human being, that the happiest effects are achieved. As in the case of the engaging and exuberant Mr. William Hickey, whose memoirs are here reviewed,* and who is the kind of person with whom Mr. Forster is, on paper, on the happiest terms.

> " As the old boy looked back at his jumble of a career and particularly at the Indian fragments of it, what significance could it have had to him ? Why, none at all, no significance at all, he is not that type of observer. He is not philosophic or profound. He just writes ahead. . . . Turn off the raptures of heaven and hell. Leave, as sole illumination for its universe, the ' extraordinary blaze of light ' that falls upon a bachelor dinner-table. . . . Off he goes without offering any opportunity for reflection, which is one of the reasons why we like him so much. He has never been pretentious or insincere ; he has never regretted or repented or said ' I have lived ' or ' I have served England in my little way,' or ' I, too, have felt the lure of the East.' How pleasant it would have been to have met him, and how strange it is to realize that one has often met him and fled from him. For he must be reincarnate to-day in many a smoking-room, many an overseas dining club or tenth-rate military mess."

This is the novelist speaking : perhaps the permanent leader of Mr. Forster's writing team ? And again, in the little story of Mr. and Mrs. Abbey, guardians of the Keats children, who in no other hands have been such overbearing,

* *Abinger Harvest.*

nagging, yet natural flesh and blood.* *A Passage to India* is Mr. Forster's only novel of the decade; but the novelist is busy through nearly all the literary criticisms, articles, and essays, even the most casual of current reviews, making portraits and characters, with a touch here, a tap there, the hint of a laugh throughout.

Here, for example, is Mrs. Hannah More,* " the god-mother of my great-aunt." A picture is described: it is " Mrs. Hannah More and favourite squirrel ":

> " They too are seated—the old lady at a Chippendale table, the squirrel upon it. They face one another, they bend their necks with identical gesture, and the calm light of a hundred years ago flows in through square panes of glass upon the letter and the nut that they are opening."

Mrs. Hannah More had, as we know, four sisters, all spinsters too:

> " Five, all attaining the age of seventy, all lively, hospitable, and jabbering, all suppressing the Slave Trade and elevating the poor. . . . What can it have been like ? It only becomes real to me in this little squirrel picture, painted when the sands were running out. Something faint and delicate emerges, the books rise to the ceiling, but the trees stir in the garden. The lovely provincialism of England takes shape, detaches itself from our suburbanism, smiles, says, ' I like my books, I like my garden, I like elevating the lower orders,' and manages not to be absurd."

The note of the essay is pleasure; and to recall for the moment the harsh words that are often

* *Abinger Harvest.*

to-day our tribute to Mrs. Hannah and her kind is to realize again that Mr. Forster is not a writer specifically of to-day at all, but one with roots in every past. He gives Mrs. Hannah credit for understanding something about the poor whom she educated, with whose lives she interfered.

> " She shared their sentimentality, and that love of anniversaries and funerals which supplies the absence of Art, and though she checked the vice which was their chief solace, she was not wild or stupid about it ; she could even accept help from ' a woman of loose morals but good natural sense, who became our friend sooner than some of the decent and the formal ' . . . Around her house for a radius of many miles the faint glimmer of education spread—samplers and alphabets, the sparks of our present conflagration."

Hannah More, William Hickey, Mr. and Mrs. Abbey, Trooper Comberbacke,* the Emperor Babur,* Wilfred Blunt,* the genial filibustering Sir Wallis Budge,* the angry romantic Ibsen,* Proust,* with his indefatigable curiosity and his despair—there they all are, a gallery of living beings, as real as if they were in novels, and relieved of the necessity of paying that attention to one another that is the novelist's burden and bane. These beings can each pursue his and her own destiny, bombinating most pleasurably for us through the clear and irradiating window panes that beautify and magnify and impart so pleasant a comic skew.

* *Abinger Harvest.*

Among these personal appreciations, these miniature novels, there is an interesting fragment of literary speculation, a pamphlet of 1925 called *Anonymity. An Enquiry*. The enquiry is, Do you like to know who a book's by ? and it develops into an essay on the function of words—words as conveying information, as creating atmosphere, as expressing, or, alternatively, transcending, personality. All literature, all creative and poetic literature, that is, " tends towards a condition of anonymity, and, so far as words are creative, a signature merely distracts us from their true significance "—that is the contention. For such literature comes from " the lower personality," into which creative writers must dip their buckets. Creation comes from the depths; style and personality, the signed stuff, are of the surface. Information about facts, newspaper articles, should be signed; poetry should not, for it is universal, and speaks to man's soul, its source is the depths of the sea, where, as the essay on Ibsen puts it, romanticism lies hid. " Lost in the beauty where the poet was lost," we forget the speaker and remember only the Word.

An elusive hare is thus started and pursued. It is possible to hold that even the sublimest beauty is signed without detriment to its universality ; that the *Ancient Mariner*, rising like a magnificent phosphorescent fish from the deep strange seas of Coleridge's rich imagination and miscellaneous reading, loses no quality of generalness or of beauty by being inalienably Coleridge's and no other's. The theme is obviously limitlessly debatable. Mr. Forster, as a poet and mystic, comes down on one side; as stylist and individualist, he might likely enough, on some other occasion, take the other. *Anonymity* is, anyhow, an exciting piece of speculation.

# CHAPTER XIV

## ASPECTS OF THE NOVEL

NOVELISTS must, one supposes, be interested in the art of the novel. So it is natural
that Mr. Forster should, in 1927, have delivered
the Clark lectures at Cambridge on this subject.
They were published under the name *Aspects of
the Novel*.

Though, owing to their subject, Mr. Forster's
(to me) least interesting book, they represent, in a
sense, his highest feat, for he has really made of this
rather tedious topic what is, though with limitations, a good, stimulating and witty philosophic
monograph. Other people have written delightful
novels, brilliant essays, even entertaining guide
books; but to give lectures at once amusing,
imaginative, and scholarly on " The Novel "
(is it the " The " that is so daunting ?)—well,
Sir Walter Raleigh did it, but I know not who
besides; and even Professor Raleigh was more
orthodox in treatment, more of the professional
scholar and don. Here, approaching this " formidable mass," this " spongy tract," the English
novel, is a mind whose critical apparatus is
philosophic, speculative, sensitively aware of the

P

flickering lights and shadows of the human consciousness, of the novelists sitting, as it were, round
a room, all writing their novels at once, irrespective
of chronology. And " Let us," he says, " look
over their shoulders for a moment and see what
they are writing." Having done so, he indicates
essential resemblances between those of different
periods by grouping a few of them into pairs, and
then proceeds to discuss seven " aspects " of the
thing they are busy on—Story, People, Plot,
Fantasy and Prophecy, Pattern and Rhythm.

The story he recognizes as the first essential of
the novel, but (in often quoted words) regrets it.

> " Yes—oh dear yes—the novel tells a story. That is the
> fundamental aspect without which it could not exist . . . and
> I wish that it was not so, that it could be something different—
> melody, or perception of the truth, not this low atavistic
> form."

If the novel were melody or perception of the
truth, it would be (as Mr. Bingley said of the
suggested ball which should be all conversation)
very delightful, but not nearly so like a novel. Mr.
Forster knows this, of course, but is sorry that it
is so, for the more we look at the story, the less
shall we find to admire, in this primitive age-old
tale told round the camp-fire to a primitive audience of shockheads. What happened next—that
is the root of the matter in the primitive mind.

> " Qua story, it can only have one merit : that of making the
> audience want to know what happens next. And conversely it

can only have one fault : that of making the audience not want to know what happens next. These are the only two criticisms that can be made on the story that is a story."

(Not true, of course: the primitive audience might make the criticism that what happened next disappointed and annoyed them when they learnt it, so that they knocked the narrator on the head; the proviso should be added that what happens next must be up to standard—the standard demanded by its hearers.)

Scott, Mr. Forster goes on, tells a story, and that is all Scott does. By thinking this of Scott, he misses the best of him. Scott, besides telling a story, makes people talk—real people, real talk, once you get away from the " genteel young man " and the still more genteel young woman, and the rest of the outfit of the romantic novelist of the period. There are scenes in Scott that are dramatic, exciting, passionately felt; like the scene in *Old Mortality* when Claverhouse is watching the torturing of the Covenanter Macbriar, and in *Guy Mannering*, when the Laird of Ellengowan is cursed by Meg Merrilees. The tide scene in *The Antiquary*, which Mr. Forster quotes with disapproval, is, indeed, rather tepidly and heavily dealt with, yet I do not mind Isabella's speech:

" Must we yield life without a struggle ? Is there no path, however dreadful, by which we could climb the crag or at least attain some height above the tide. . . ."

etc. It is as agreeable and sensible a suggestion as

many made by Defoe's characters, or Richardson's or Sterne's, in emergencies equally alarming, and conceived in the idiom proper to its period. I like the picture of Isabella, quite unruffled, delivering herself of these well-chosen words, while poised, in the face of the raging sea, " upon the highest ledge of rock to which they could attain."

" *The Antiquary*," says Mr. Forster,

> " is a book in which the life in time is celebrated instinctively by the novelist, and this must lead to a slackening of emotion and shallowness of judgment, and in particular to that idiotic use of marriage as a finale."

Jane Austen also wrote books in which she celebrated instinctively the life in time. It must all depend, surely, on *how* it is celebrated, in what spirit and in what manner this toast is pledged. Perhaps with Jane Austen, too, it led to slackening of emotion, shallowness of judgment, and to the idiotic use of marriage as a finale: but this seems unsatisfactory reasoning, for why should the over-emphasis on life in time, unphilosophic though it be, shallow though it be, lead to slack emotions ? It rather should lead to the tautening and intensification of emotions, of the personal emotions that are bound up with this life and this time, and spring from our narrow and intense desires. The real reasons why Scott's emotions seem to us slack are, surely, that his was not a deeply emotional nature, nor he a highly accomplished craftsman of the emotions, that he wrote in the temperate and somewhat stilted idiom of his time, and that his genteel characters, those young gentlemen and ladies to whom it is most proper that strong emotions should occur, are, owing to an unfortunate and irritating limitation of his powers, nearly all dummies. (The only exceptions I can remember are Diana Vernon and Julia Mannering, and they are not much.)

If the lecturer seems to some critics partly confused about Scott, he seems to others (or possibly the same) not to have hit quite the right nail on the head in his reference to Miss Gertrude Stein. She has, he said, tried to

> " emancipate fiction from the tyranny of time, and to express in it the life by values only. . . . She wants to abolish this whole aspect of the story, this sequence in chronology, and my heart goes out to her. . . . It is much more important to play about like this than to rewrite the Waverley Novels. Yet the experiment is doomed to failure. The time-sequence cannot be destroyed without carrying in its ruin all that should have taken its place ; the novel that would express values only becomes unintelligible and therefore valueless."

The reason why many hearts do *not* go out to Miss Stein, is not that she has tried to abolish the time-sequence, but that she has tried to abolish something far more important—the precise and delicate use of words. About language she is a philistine, a barbarian, a Vandal, practically a butcher; and language is all the time in such dire peril from those who have no use for its delicacies, its euphonies, its exquisite felicities, its function as the conveyor of ideas, facts, emotions and sounds, that writers who bludgeon and torture it, smash it deliberately, for experiment's sake, for ignorance, or any other reason why, should have no share of good hearts, which should relegate them to the unwanted category of bulls in china shops. To smash up and uglify language is unpardonable, even if the time-sequence is smashed with the same hammer. Experiment, yes, by all means: but in a direction that will intensify the precision and significance of the delicate instrument, not in one that blunts and coarsens it, making it sound like the mouthing of the unlettered, the warbling of the native woodnotes wild of that great unfastidious company who do not connect words with any particular meanings, and do not care.

Still, Mr. Forster might well reply that he was not concerned in this connection to state the quarrel of language-lovers with Miss Stein, but only Miss Stein's relations to the time-sequence convention: he closes the first lecture with a request to us to join him " in repeating in exactly the right tone of voice," that is, " a little sadly," the essential aspects of the novel. " Yes—oh, dear, yes—the novel tells a story." Having secured our agreement to this, and secured from some of us the right tone, from others the wrong (for there will be a large school of readers who will cry joyfully, " Yes, thank God, it does.

Thank God for the enthralling stories of *Howards End*, *A Passage to India*, *A Room With a View*, *The Longest Journey* ")—the lecturer proceeds to People.

Here " the novelist will be appealing to our intelligence and imagination, not merely to our curiosity." " We need not ask what happened next, but to whom did it happen."

And here again we must register a protest, for the novelist, by telling us " what happened next," should appeal to our intelligence and imagination, as much as when he tells us to whom it happened. What happened next may be something that it requires much more intelligence and imagination to apprehend and appreciate than to whom it happened, which is usually of greater interest to the somewhat elementary minds of not highly educated young ladies. One can imagine the circle of " shock-headed listeners " sitting over the camp-fire clutching their gnawed bones, hearing the story-teller flow on; one can fancy a different emphasis of interest among the male and female listeners, gruff voices asking " What happened then ? " shrill voices chirping in with " Who, Who ? What were they like ? " Still, in both curiosities, the highest intelligences and the lowest can meet; it depends, as everything else does, on how the thing is done. What happened to Satan in *Paradise Lost*, when from morn to noon he fell, from noon to dewy eve, a summer's day, needs no personal interest to give it imaginative value; the beauty is in the magnificently described and matchless event, though enhanced by the knowledge that the superb decadent is proud Lucifer. On the other hand, the ball at Netherfield would be but a trivial piece of social gossip if unlit by our interest in the personalities who footed it there.

Still, when all is said, a novel must deal with people. " The actors in a story are, or pretend to be, human beings." Mr. Forster briefly tabulates the main facts in the life of a human being, of Homo Sapiens, and enquires how far these are reproduced in Homo Fictus. The answer is, of course, that several of the main functions of humanity—such as truth, food, sleep, death—are but cursorily dealt with, while love gets more than its share of attention.

> " The constant sensitiveness of characters for each other—even in writers called robust like Fielding—is remarkable, and has no parallel in life, except among people who have plenty of leisure. Passion, intensity at moments—yes, but not this constant awareness, this endless readjusting, this ceaseless hunger. I believe that these are the reflections of the novelist's own state of mind while he composes, and that the predominance of love in novels is partly because of this."

And partly because love, illusorily regarded by both novelist and reader as a permanency, ends a book conveniently, and this though—

> " All history, all our experience, teaches us that no human relationship is constant, it is as unstable as the living beings

who compose it, and they must balance like jugglers if it is to remain ; if it is constant it is no longer a human relationship but a social habit, the emphasis in it has passed from love to marriage. All this we know, yet we cannot bear to apply our bitter knowledge to the future. . . . Any strong emotion brings with it the illusion of permanence, and the novelists have seized upon this. They usually end their books with marriage, and we do not object because we lend them our dreams."

So, then, Homo Fictus is generally born off, sometimes dies on, wants little food or sleep, is tirelessly occupied with human relationships. (Or, Mr. Forster might have added, but did not, with constant adventurous deeds of daring, for Homo Fictus is often a hazardous kind of a man, endowed with super-human powers of resilience and pertinacity.)

But the most important thing about Homo Fictus, as distinguished from Homo Sapiens, is that he is a more manageable creature, for his creator and we can know all about him. A character in a book is " real " when the novelist knows everything about it.

" He will give us the feeling that though the character has not been explained, it is explicable, and we get from this a reality of a kind we can never get in daily life. . . . In this direction fiction is truer than history, because it goes beyond the evidence. . . . And that is why novels, even when they are about wicked people, can solace us ; they suggest a more comprehensible and thus a more manageable human race."

Yet this fictional human race, these " real " characters, are divided into " flat " and " round."

234 THE WRITINGS OF E. M. FORSTER

> " 'The really flat character can be expressed in one sentence such as ' I will never desert Mr. Micawber.' . . . Or ' I must conceal, even by subterfuges, the poverty of my master's house.' There is Caleb Balderstone in *The Bride of Lammermoor*. He does not use the actual phrase, but it completely describes him ; he has no existence outside it, no pleasures, none of the private lusts and aches that must complicate the most consistent of servitors. Whatever he does, wherever he goes, whatever lies he tells or plates he breaks, it is to conceal the poverty of his master's house. It is not his *idée fixe*, because there is nothing in him into which the idea can be fixed. He is the idea, and such life as he possesses radiates from its edges and from the scintillations it strikes when other elements in the novel impinge."

But the flat character is generously accorded his great merit—he is easily recognized by the reader whenever he comes in.

> " In Russian novels, where they so seldom occur, they would be a decided help. It is a convenience for an author when he can strike with his full force at once, and flat characters are very useful to him, since they never need reintroducing, never run away, have not to be watched for development, and provide their own atmosphere . . . most satisfactory."

Flat characters move through the book undeveloping and unchanged; moreover, we remember them easily, and like them, for " all of us, even the sophisticated, yearn for permanence, and to the unsophisticated permanence is the chief excuse for a work of art."

The critic's complaint against the flat character is summed up in the words of Mr. Norman Douglas to D. H. Lawrence, complaining that he, in a biography of a friend, has falsified the picture by employing " the novelist's touch." Yet, says Mr. Forster, a novel often requires flat people as well as round. Dickens, for example: " his immense success with types suggests that there may be more in flatness than the severer critics admit." For Dickens gets away with it.

> " Probably the immense vitality of Dickens causes his characters to vibrate a little, so that they borrow his life and appear to lead one of their own. . . . Good but imperfect novelists, like Wells and Dickens, are very clever at transmitting force. The part of their novel that is alive galvanizes the part that is not, and causes the characters to jump about and speak in a convincing way. They are quite different from the perfect novelist who touches all his material directly, who seems to pass the creative finger down every sentence and into every word. Richardson, Defoe, Jane Austen, are perfect in this particular way."

All Jane Austen's characters, says Mr. Forster, are round. And Richardson's. This seems a little odd. Is Lovelace, is Clarissa, a round, realized human being ? But this question of flatness and roundness, of where the outline of rotundity wobbles and slips away into nebulous amorphousness or becomes merely the blank circle of the O, the nought, the ball which is bowled arbitrarily through the hoops of happenings, without character, colours, or life of its own, all this question, in fact, of the nature of roundness, is debatable, subjective, and complicated. One man's round character will be another's empty, bowling ball.

Mr. Forster's enquiries into the business light the mind; but the judgment in each particular case each reader has to make for himself, for it is essentially a personal matter, and will depend partly on how much the reader, through his own contacts and experience and temper, knows about the character of whom he reads; and this is, to the novelist, an incalculable factor in transmission. For one reader, not all the novelist's skill and imaginative creation will avail to push a particular character into his realization; for the next, it is done with a casual touch and no skill required. This is apparent whenever novels and the people in them are discussed among a group of intelligent readers.

After people, the lecturer deals with Plot, which he defines as " a narrative of events, the emphasis falling on causality," whereas a story is " a narrative of events arranged in their time-sequence." The distinction is neatly illustrated:

> " ' The king died and then the queen died,' is a story. ' The king died and then the queen died of grief' is a plot. The time-sequence is preserved, but the sense of causality overshadows it. Or again : ' The queen died, no one knew why, until it was discovered that it was through grief at the death of the king.' This is a plot with a mystery in it, a form capable of high development. . . . Consider the death of the queen. If it is in a story we say ' and then ? ' If it is in a plot we ask ' why ? ' That is the fundamental difference between these two aspects of the novel."

It could not be more succinctly put. But it goes on,

" A plot cannot be told to a gaping audience of cave men or to a tyrannical sultan or to their modern descendant the movie-public. They can only be kept awake by ' and then—and then '—they can only supply curiosity. But a plot demands intelligence and memory also."

and this is more questionable. The cave man, the sultan, and certainly the movie-public (of which most of us, at one time or another, form part) enjoy plot; a mystery is one of the surest stimulants to the primitive human mind; it appeals to its curiosity. And here, I think, Mr. Forster is confused. Obviously a mystery, or a plot, appeals to curiosity. Yet he goes on: " Curiosity is one of the lowest of the human faculties. You will have noticed in daily life that when people are inquisitive, they nearly always have bad memories and are usually stupid at bottom." But this surely depends on what they are inquisitive about. Darwin was inquisitive about earth worms; Newton about why apples fall earthward; Watts about why steam comes out of the kettle; Bacon about whether snow would preserve a dead hen; Socrates about human motives; Proust about life, love, and art: in short, the point is hardly worth making that curiosity, even if it kills the cat, has produced most forms of human intellectual activity. The inquisitive child, asking perpetually: " Why, why, why ? " is troublesome, but one would not have him otherwise. Curiosity, says Mr. Forster, does not take us far into the novel—

only as far as the story. But why not into the mysteries of the plot, and the motives of the characters ? It is apparent that Mr. Forster is using " curiosity," that fine word, in some de-based sense, which divorces it from intelligence. For, as he goes on to say, " if we would grasp the plot, we must add intelligence and memory."

The comments on plot that follow, and the illustrations that point them, are excellent talk. The relation, the incurably awkward relation, between the characters in a novel and the plot which they have to assist in constructing, is the main theme. Death and marriage, he observes, are about the average novelist's only connection between his characters and his plot.

And why, he goes on to ask, has a novel to have a plot, to be planned ? Couldn't it grow ? Modern writers say that fiction can devise another and a more suitable framework. He instances Gide's *Les Faux Monnayeurs*, which attempts to fit something else in the place of plot.

It is a stimulating theme : but on the whole the least successful of the series, being more chatty than coherent; possibly because plot is of less interest to the lecturer than his other heads; he gives, somehow, the impression of forcing himself at a five-barred gate, and then giving up and walking round it instead, hurrying on to the next field, which is called Fantasy and Prophecy, and is much more agreeable to his horse's paces.

But no, Fantasy and Prophecy are not fields, they are the light that illuminates the fields.

> " There is more in the novel than time or people or logic. . . . And by ' more ' I do not mean something that excludes these aspects, nor something that includes them and embraces them. I mean something that cuts across them like a bar of light, that is intimately connected with them at one place and patiently illumines all their problems, and at another place shoots over or through them as if they did not exist. We shall give that bar of light two names, fantasy and prophecy."

Fantasy " asks us to pay something extra," to accept something that could not occur. Fantasy and Prophecy are alike in introducing gods, but they introduce different gods, the one a flight of light-weight, mischievous, come-and-go creatures, such as dryads, fairies, fauns, and odd chances and accidents, the other a divinity (is that the collective noun ?) of great, fateful and awful beings. Fantasy may deal with the super-normal, with witches, ghosts and gods, but need not; it may merely imply an odd, freakish attitude, as in *Tristram Shandy*, or *Zuleika Dobson*. Joyce's *Ulysses* is brought, perhaps a little arbitrarily, into this section; Mr. Forster seems conscious of an imperfect fit here, but includes it " because the raging of Joyce, like the happier or calmer moods of the other writers, seems essentially fantastic."

This extension of the limits of fantasy might have been carried to further lengths; there is a fantastic element in a great deal of " straight fiction " which might have been touched on, for it is a subject particularly suited to the lecturer. He takes us through it rather too quickly—one has to remember that they *were* lectures, and time was short—and gets on to Prophecy, which is Fantasy with a grander mythology. Prophecy in a novel

> " is an accent in the novelist's voice, an accent for which the flutes and saxophones of fantasy may have prepared us. His theme is the universe, or something universal, but he is not necessarily going to ' say ' anything about the universe ; he proposes to sing, and the strangeness of song arising in the halls of fiction is bound to give us a shock. How will song combine with the furniture of common sense ? we shall ask ourselves, and shall have to answer ' not too well ' : the singer does not always have room for gestures, the tables and chairs get broken, and the novel through which bardic influence has passed often has a wrecked air, like a drawing-room after an earthquake or a children's party. Readers of D. H. Lawrence will understand what I mean.
>
> " Prophecy—in our sense—is a tone of voice. It may imply any of the faiths that have haunted humanity—Christianity, Buddhism, dualism, Satanism, or the mere raising of human love and hatred to such a power that their normal receptacles no longer contain them."

To understand the prophetic aspect, we must put on humility, and suspend the sense of humour.

> " Like the school-children in the Bible, one cannot help laughing at a prophet—his bald head is so absurd—but one can discount the laughter and realize that it has no critical value and is merely food for bears."

Dostoevsky is a prophet; so are Herman

Melville, D. H. Lawrence and Emily Brontë.
Dostoevsky reaches back to universal pity and love.
*Moby Dick*—

> " Nothing can be stated about *Moby Dick* except that it is
> a contest. The rest is song. It is to his conception of evil that
> Melville's work owes much of its strength."

D. H. Lawrence is

> " the only prophetic novelist writing to-day—all the rest are
> fantasists or preachers : the only living novelist in whom the
> song predominates, who has the rapt bardic quality, and whom
> it is idle to criticize."

Yet he preaches, he bullies, he nags, and " humility is not easy with this irritable and irritating
author," whose greatness lies far back, resting on
something æsthetic. " What is valuable about him
cannot be put into words; it is colour, gesture and
outline in people and things."

This is profoundly true: but it leaves one not
quite certain whether Lawrence's æsthetic greatness is connected with his prophetic gift, his
" rapt bardic quality," or whether Mr. Forster
regards it as the pearl found in the dung-hill, the
dung-hill being the prophecy and preaching. One
gathers that he does so regard it, but also accepts
the fact that the æsthetic creativeness is bound up
with the other, and could not be reached except by
this tiresome path.

As to *Wuthering Heights*, though it contains no
view of the universe, tempest and explosions fill it,
" and only in confusion could the figures of

Q

Heathcliff and Catherine externalize their passion till it streamed through the house and over the moors." Emily Brontë was a prophetess, " because what is implied is more important to her than what is said." But she might, I think, with her concentrated local passion, more rightly be classed as a poet. One questions Mr. Forster's admission that " no great book is more cut off from the universals of Heaven and Hell." It is possible, on the contrary, to regard its passions and their human embodiments, as outriders from Heaven and from Hell. But a certain weariness possesses the lecturer through this theme; a sense of inconsistency, of, as he says, a reservation, of having to use, for the purpose of assessing the prophetic aspect, a different and more defective set of tools. The novel has soared up into a less accessible sphere, and our spy-glasses get only partial glimpses of it there.

For the next lecture it is brought within reach of inspection again; its pattern and rhythm are now studied. To illustrate pattern, there is *Thais*, in the shape of an hour-glass (the two agonists approaching one another from afar, meeting in the middle of the book, crossing and receding, each to the other's former spiritual plane) and there is Percy Lubbock's *Roman Pictures*, shaped like the grand chain in the Lancers (the central figure meets a friend, and then sets out to make a number of other social contacts in turn, until, the circle

complete, he meets his original partner again).
Pattern, it will be seen, "springs mainly from the
plot." Henry James's *Ambassadors* is also hour-
glass in shape, the two principal characters meeting in the book's centre, in a unity both local and
spiritual, then diverging, and, in a sense, changing
places. The pattern is formal and exquisite, and,
to achieve it, as to achieve all his patterns, James
has had to sacrifice half the humanity of his cast.

> " The characters, besides being few in number, are con-
> structed on very stingy lines. They are incapable of fun, of
> rapid motion, of carnality, and of nine-tenths of heroism.
> Their clothes will not take off, the diseases that ravage them
> are anonymous, like the sources of their income. . . . Even
> their sensations are limited. They can land in Europe and
> look at works of art and at each other, but that is all. Maimed
> creatures can alone breathe in Henry James's pages—maimed
> yet specialized. . . . Now this drastic curtailment . . . is in
> the interests of the pattern."

Can the weaving of a deliberate and rigid pattern
be combined with the richness of the material
which life provides ? Mr. Forster's answer is
that it cannot:

> " a rigid pattern . . . shuts the doors on life and leaves the
> novelist doing exercises, generally in the drawing-room. . . .
> To most readers of fiction the sensation from a pattern is not
> intense enough to justify the sacrifices that made it, and their
> verdict is ' Beautifully done, but not worth doing.' "

Then Rhythm. As in a musical symphony,
there is the easy rhythm of parts, and the more
difficult, less apprehensible rhythm of the whole.

The first is to be found in Proust, chaotic and ill-constructed though this whole is. Is the second to be found anywhere ?

> " Is there any effect in novels comparable to the effect of the Fifth Symphony as a whole, where when the orchestra stops, we hear something that has actually never been played ? The opening movement, the andante, and the trio-scherzo-trio-finale-trio-finale that composes the third block, all enter the mind at once, and extend one another into a common entity. This common entity, this new thing, is the symphony as a whole . . . I cannot find any analogy. Yet there may be one; in music fiction is likely to find its nearest parallel. . . . Music . . . does offer in its final expression a type of beauty which fiction might achieve in its own way. Expansion. That is the idea the novelist must cling to."

He finds something of this rhythmic quality, this expansion and liberation, in *War and Peace*.

> " Such an untidy book. Yet, as we read it, do not great chords begin to sound behind us, and when we have finished does not every item—even the catalogue of strategies—lead a larger existence than was possible at the time ? "

*War and Peace* is his only example. But it is possible to find precisely this quality in other novels; some find it in Conrad, some in Hardy, some in Meredith; I have known those who found it in George Eliot. The rhythm of a symphony or of a literary work are alike only audible to the individual ear and brain, and these make of what they hear and of what they read whatever it is possible and suitable that they should make; there are laws that direct works of art and quite other laws that govern their reception by our varying human intelligences and sensibilities, so that one man's great symphony (musical or other) will be the next man's facile rubbish, and so forth. All this makes of art a very confused but pleasing business, like a confused rich meal at which all kinds of different tastes and appetites eat and drink. " A fine, full, rich wine," one will say: " when you drink it, great chords begin to sound, and when you have finished it everything in life seems to have a larger existence than before." " Rubbishy stuff," says his neighbour after trying it. " Chords, indeed! If you want a really fine, strong, splendid drink, try this. . . ." And so on, and so on—to each his symphony, but attained by different symbols. Mr. Forster would, probably, admit this, which in no way vitiates discussion of the technique of art, but discounts attempts at analysing too closely its effects on our poor wavering minds.

The lectures end with a few speculations. The future of the novel. It will not essentially alter, not alter except in externals, and of course in technique, unless human beings learn to look at themselves in a new way, and therefore to set down quite new things about human life; unless they extend that " shy crab-like sideways movement " of the human mind out of the forward onrush of history, until it revolutionizes human movement.

Throwing out this characteristic suggestion, the lecturer concludes; or rather ceases.

One is left with the feeling of the turning up of new paths on this well-worn, this much-travelled country, enquiry into the novel—the traveller, not having a one-track mind, wobbles a little on the road, looks over hedges, gets over stiles into uncut fields where he proceeds to make footpaths. In doing so, he encounters objects which detain him; they are off the path, they perhaps grow in a hedge or shine in a ditch, but he lingers with them, forgetting for a time his path. As for example, when he pauses in his analysis of the " pattern " of *The Ambassadors*, to give us the amusing description of " Mamie," and of the correspondence between Henry James and H. G. Wells about *Boon*. His illustrations often lead him too far out of his road, and he cannot always quite get back again, for time is short. But his paths, when he will stay on them, beguile and enchant, take us across the odd, amorphous swampy country, in and out of thickets and orchards and across plains, up and down hills, in a way exciting to the imagination. And, taking them by and large, the paths do radiate out from and return to the main road, along which we are exploring the relation between the two forces, " human beings and a bundle of various things not human beings," and the novelist's business of adjusting these two forces and conciliating their claims. There are, of course, many aspects of the novel not touched on: the analysis is selective, not exhaustive; in six short lectures, it could not be otherwise; the hare is started, and left not exhausted but startled to fresh life. It is an uneven book, full of excitements and opening doors and sudden flaggings and peterings out, and thin bits, as if some aspect of the affair suddenly became too tangled for further investigation and must be left at that.

# CHAPTER XV

TO lecture on the novel may be a mistake for a novelist, daunting the lecturer from doing any more with that amorphous Protean form than enquire into its destinies, functions and problems. Who, as Horace Walpole remarked, would ever have wrote a novel who had considered the matter gravely ? Be that as it may, Mr. Forster has, as we know, published no more novels since he did thus consider their aspects. But he has continued his series of what I will call novelettes; essays, that is, on persons.

One of the most agreeable of these is the *Letter to Madan Blanchard*, that eccentric mariner who deserted his shipmates and captain and remained behind on a Pacific island in the year 1783. He stayed behind, and Lee Boo, a young black prince, sailed away with the ship's company to be reared in England. This charming and ingenuous blackamoor, the excellent Captain who took charge of him, and Blanchard, the enigmatic sailor who went native on a Pellew island, are the heroes of the letter, or the novelette, or the philosophic speculation, or the nostalgic fantasy, whichever one likes to call it. The chief hero is Blanchard. For,

> "The people who touch my imagination are obstinate suddenly—they do break step and I always hope they'll get by without the sergeant punishing them. . . . If it isn't one set of rules it's another. . . . I ought to feel free myself, as I've health, strength, and am middle-aged, yet I can't keep my hat on in a church, for instance. . . . While not getting fussed over this, I can't but remember the people who managed better, and it's in order to meet them in the flesh that I study history. Here and there, as I rake between the importancies, I come across them—the people who carried whimsicality into action, the salt of my earth. Not the professional whimsies— their drill's drearier than anyone's—but the solid fellows who suddenly jib. The queer thing is we all admire them. . . . They've got hold of something which we know is there, but have never dared to grasp in our hands. A sort of stinging nettle."

The fellows who suddenly jib: he has written of many of them: Stephen Wonham, who threw off even the clothes that old Mrs. Failing had given him, swam a stream, and jibbed into poverty and freedom; Paul Gauguin, who " sacrificed everything to his art," " gave up his bank and his family and drifted to Tahiti, then, going further still, went native in the Marquesas Islands. He left nothing behind him there except some canvases, an armful of bastards, and a little carving "; the Chevalier de la Barre, who omitted to salute a religious procession and was beheaded for it; Trooper Comberbacke, the hero of one of the most entertaining novelettes,* who ran away from

* *Abinger Harvest.*

Cambridge and enlisted as a trooper, was bought out, returned to Cambridge, ran away again, and three years later wrote *The Ancient Mariner*: it is such jibbers as these whom he most likes. Eccentrics; oddities, who take their own way and diverge. Joan of Arc, Gaudier-Brzeska, Cowper, Voltaire,* T. E. Lawrence,* Hannah More,* Edward Gibbon in the Hampshire militia,* Marie Corelli hoarding sugar to make jam, doing her illegal Bit in the Great War—these are the subjects of his attention and his pen. When he has occasion to deal with those who like to enforce orthodoxy, such as Mr. Belloc (whose history of England he reviews with distaste, even with detestation) he ceases to smile, he grows apprehensive, caustic, and what he calls fussed. Even the good-humoured G. K. Chesterton, whom he rather likes, thus stirs his distaste. He is never at ease with totalitarians, whether religious or political. These two eminent and gifted Roman Catholics could both themselves jib and be eccentric, but they condemned a certain kind of mental jibbing, a jibbing from the creed which they held, and their vigorous intolerance, and what he regarded as Mr. Belloc's slippery use of history, makes Mr. Forster, with his libertolatry and his regard for intellectual integrity, see as nearly red as may be. They are not his kind: with a few chilly and impatient words he turns from them, to describe

* *Abinger Harvest.*

a pageant of Living Chess at Cracow,* or the Strat-
ford Jubilee of 1769, or the eye-shaped windows
in the roofs of a Rumanian town, or Mickey and
Minnie,* or the letters of Jane Austen.* He does
not much like these letters; his criticisms, indeed,
are a good example of his refusal to be imposed on
by a reputation; but Jane Austen, at her least
admirable, was anyhow not trying to bully the
world into acceptance of a view; she often wrote
trivially, even at times wrote waspishly, but she
was not making a case, she was not trying, as the
militant religious and militant political so often
will, to put something across us. What jars in her
letters is her occasional lack of good feeling. For
triviality, giggling, perpetual officers and balls,
she could be forgiven; but not for cruel jests such
as

"'Mrs. Hall was brought to bed yesterday of a dead child,
some weeks before she expected, owing to a fright. I suppose
she happened unawares to look at her husband.' Did Cassandra laugh? Probably, but all that we can catch at this
distance is the whinnying of harpies."

Not fair on Cassandra, of course: one might
equally easily say that she probably did not laugh,
but replied, "Jane, how can you be so unkind?"
and that Jane repented. That is the worst of publishing the letters of the dead, they grin and stare
and grimace and scowl at us, expressing for ever,
in black ink on paper, moods which were scarcely

* Abinger Harvest.

even moods, so glibly did they run by, run off the pen. *Lapsus calami:* they are often lapses indeed, and probably no letters should be kept. The impact of Jane's on Mr. Forster is " triviality, varied by touches of ill-breeding and of sententiousness." Their fundamental weakness is that their writer " had not enough subject-matter on which to exercise her powers," their strength is family affection. Mr. Forster makes her the heroine of one of his novelettes (the article is a review of the Oxford Press edition of her letters, 1932);* but, unlike most of his heroes and heroines, he does not like her much, nor love her at all; she was no jibber, and he cannot feel for her the warmth that he feels for the eccentrics, even for such mild eccentrics as Crabbe and Cowper, or the erratic Mr. Ford Madox Ford.

But through the 1930's one sees advancing a significant change in emphasis. These literary, historical and personal appreciations, these vignettes that I have called novelettes, because their main interest is in human creatures, so that even a review of a book on a Napoleonic campaign becomes a picture of the characteristic whimsies of a great buccaneering human oddity—these interests are being elbowed a little aside by those more formidable preoccupations which seize and hold us to-day; preoccupations with the fearful state of this present world in which we so

* *Abinger Harvest*

precariously live. War, peace, freedom, culture, less in culture's proper sense of a civilized equipment of thought and art, than in the newer sense it has lately developed of " the fight against Fascism "—these are the fires that burn in us to-day, and which kindle in Mr. Forster the flames of apprehensive passion. He is not naturally politically minded; he can and does, unlike some democrats to-day, write an article on what he holds is the rapid and shocking present decadence of culture in its strict sense, for culture in this sense is the thing, next to freedom, that is nearest his heart. Indeed, his apprehensions as to its fate make him exaggerate its present plight; a comparison of the size of the audiences at performances of Shakespeare, at classical concerts (and the B.B.C., which he blames for much, has done good work in training its clientèle to listen to good music, in the intervals between jazz bands, crooners, and baritones who want to go down to the sea) and of the numbers of people who read what is vaguely called " good literature," would not, I think, induce pessimism. We pessimize about culture because there is more vulgar stuff produced and enjoyed than before, owing to new facilities for its production and to an increasing public just educated up to enjoying it but no farther. There are more jazz bands, more crooners, more vulgar plays and films, books and newspapers, than ever before in history; there are also more good concerts, good films, and for all I know good " stills " painted (this, I understand, is the correct name to-day for such pictures as are incapable of motion). There is probably a higher general level of culture than before the last war; it will never be high, general levels never are; there is also a flooding swamp of cheerfully complacent vulgarity, and, as the Queen of Heaven gloomily observed to King Alfred in Chesterton's ballad, the flood rises higher. It rises so high, and its smell is so bad, that Mr. Forster fears lest it should submerge the cultural world and drown what he values most. So, in 1935, he writes dejectedly on the dwindling of culture.

There is no political implication in this article. But a week later (he is writing " Notes on the Way " in *Time and Tide*) he opens with the horrid word " War," and proceeds

" It must occur to everyone at moments that it is futile to be interested in Parliament, the countryside, art and literature, social reform, personal relationships, or any of the subjects which attract decent people : futile because they rest on a crust which may break beneath us to-morrow."

There follows an admirable article (its views will be summarized in the final section of this book) on the various attitudes that it is possible to adopt towards war and its prevention. That minds such as his should discuss subjects such as this is vital and essential. But it is an article not recognizably signed; it might be by some other intelligent, rational and sensitive writer. Probably because his usual style, however seriously he is writing, is largely compact of humour, fancy, and allusiveness, and these dark and grim subjects give little scope for such graces. The same applies, more or less, to articles on threats to freedom, on Fascism, Communism, the Aldershot Tattoo, the Sedition Bill, and other menacing shapes; in all of them he speaks with the voice of cultured, sensitive and democratic liberalism rather than with his own peculiar note, or rather, he is speaking with that part of his voice which sings in the choir with cultured, sensitive and democratic liberalism. Its dominant song is of liberty, of passionate revolt against tyranny and cruelty, of hatred for such political creeds as make for these. Distaste for the regimentation, the crudity and the violence of communism fights with a belief that communism may possibly be the only way to save the world.

In 1934, in the midst of all the alarms and the tragedies that haunt " the sinister corridor of our age," he has a Note on the Way on Matthew Arnold's question: " Who prop, thou ask'st, in these bad days, my mind ? " He answers it— the creators of beauty do; the creators of music, poetry, prose, which have given us great pleasure, not by their philosophy or good advice, but by being exquisite. Beethoven, for example. And

Matthew Arnold; not his great didactic poems, but his lyrics.

> " Literature as a retreat is rightly discredited ; it is both selfish and foolish to bury one's head in the flowers. But herbs grow in the garden too, and share in its magics, and from them is distilled the stoicism which we badly need to-day. Uneducated people have a quantity of valuable resources which are denied to people like ourselves, on whom much money has been spent, but that is no reason why we should despise our proper stock in trade."

Such consolations may work; or, on given occasions, they may not; but they are, anyhow, a chance.

The corridor grows more sinister, the skies grow darker yet; writers find it more and more difficult to keep that detachment in which emotion and art can achieve their proper balance. Amusements, ironies, purely literary interests, appear to sensitive minds like Neronic fiddlings, in the glare of those licking flames that surround our flimsy pale. Mr. Forster's attitude towards the horrid situation will be discussed later. It seems likely that its immediacy intensified for him after he had spent a year in comparative withdrawment of mind, writing the life of Goldsworthy Lowes Dickinson, which was begun in 1932 and published in 1934.

# CHAPTER XVI

## BIOGRAPHY

THE writing of the biography of a relation or close friend is one of the most difficult literary jobs. Intimacy, long and close knowledge, affection, appreciation, common language and thought, may blunt the edge of objectivity, obscure that sharp clear light which should illustrate the figure studied, and the resulting portrait may turn out no more than an affectionate gossiping reminiscence, edges and whimsies and warts smoothed away, as in those sugared memoirs of eminent men by their wives which have always so greatly abounded. Piety is a handicap. Many writers could write good lives of their grandparents; how few of their parents! The last has been done; but sometimes at the cost of gravely displeasing such parent as may remain. Most filial biographies are, as Mr. Forster remarks in his introduction to the Oxford Press edition of *The Life of Crabbe* by his son,

> "monuments of piety, beneath which the dead lie prone, never to re-arise. Nothing kills like reverence, it is the cruellest tribute one can pay to the deceased, and the reputation of Tennyson, for instance, is only just recovering from the crushing 'Life' deposited on him by his son. Such lifes should be entitled deaths."

Probably, for a successful biography, some of the novelist's showier gifts are needed; such as wit, imagination, keen observation, apt turns of phrase, sense of form, interest in character. All these E. M. Forster brought to Goldsworthy Lowes Dickinson's biography, besides intimate knowledge of the background, common experiences, appreciation, and adeptness at that small and lively detail which weaves a gay rococo pattern over the structure of narrative and thought. The result is a vivid picture, full of animation, light and shade; a decorative and beautiful picture, like the Roger Fry portrait. Its painter is, he tells us in his Epilogue, painting it because he wants to; because his friend was " beloved, affectionate, unselfish, witty, charming, inspiring," and because

> " these qualities were fused into such an unusual creature that no one whom one has met with in the flesh or in history in the least resembles it, and no words exist in which to define it. He was an indescribably rare being. . . . He did not merely increase our experience : he left us more alert for what has not yet been experienced, and more hopeful about other men because he had lived. And a biography of him, if it succeeded, would resemble him ; it would achieve the unattainable, express the inexpressible, turn the passing into the everlasting. . . . Perhaps it could only be done through music."

It might: but there is a danger of attributing to music more power than any one art can have. Music can express what is inexpressible in words, words can express what is inexpressible in music;

music can give backgrounds and undertones and symphonies of thought and passion, can report on the immortal real and reveal the spirit; but words can convey fragments and detail, those rich phenomenal felicities and humours which are equally the human being's outfit, and harder to get across to those who have not known the human being in the flesh.

In both kinds of transmission this biography seems to me to have succeeded. Certainly its subject lives as a " character," a noble, characteristic, interesting and entertaining human being, his roots firmly in the Fellows' Garden of King's, his branches reaching out to universal interests and ideas. And certainly we do get the overtones, the spiritual essence. The detail is brilliant. The record of childhood and school is written largely from Dickinson's own unpublished " Recollections "; it is interesting to notice the coincidence of comments on life at Charterhouse with those in *The Longest Journey* on Sawston school.

> " I curse the time as I look back on it. It seems to me all evil and no good. Cut off from home life and they from me, without a root to hold all that really sprang from myself . . . alone as I have never been since, physically unfit, mentally undeveloped—was ever a sadder, drearier, more hopeless entry upon life ? And no one knew. And so, of course, no one cared."

Cambridge, too. Dickinson " had no idea what Cambridge meant " when he went up there,

" and I remember," says Mr. Forster, " having the same lack of comprehension about the place myself, when my own turn came to go up there. It seems too good to be real." The experience that followed of the " magic quality " of Cambridge, too, is the same.

The similarity does not, of course, go so very far. Lowes Dickinson was essentially of his generation, rooted in the nineteenth century, a growth of Victorian intellectualism. Morgan Forster was essentially of a later time, a later culture; they read rather differently, they wrote entirely differently. " One of my limitations in discussing Dickinson is that the three writers who meant most to him have never particularly appealed to me, so that I can only divine by analogy what he found in them." There is, all the same, an admirable chapter on the three (Shelley, Plato and Goethe); as also on other matters more or less outside the biographer's experience, such as extension lecturing, medical training, politics, social work, and even psychical research.

Still, first and last, and with all its various side lines, this is the life of one member of King's College, Cambridge (both had been Fellows), by another. Beneath all the differences, the intellectual, æsthetic, political and ethical outlook are much the same, and the book gains thus a partly autobiographical interest, apart from the experiences shared together, such as the expedition to India of 1912.

Lowes Dickinson was a don, hating donnishness as only a don can; he even mistrusted research, that pure intellectual indulgence, for a reason which his biographer himself might give, " because research atrophies the mind and renders it incapable of human intercourse." Not true, of course: a hundred examples confute him; but to be rendered incapable of human intercourse was his bogy.

> " The spectacle of learning gets more depressing to me every year" (he tells Mrs. Webb). " I care only for fruitful and vital handling of the eternal commonplaces, or else for a new insight that will really help some one to internal freedom."

Fruitful and vital handling of the eternal commonplaces. The phrase recalls another, uttered in my hearing by another King's don, who greatly loved and esteemed Dickinson, and perhaps gave human intercourse as high a place, but was not much given to discussion of life. " A chatterbox," he was heard tolerantly and amiably to murmur. " Dickinson is rather a *chatterbox.*" Which is, after all, only another way of describing fruitful and vital handling of the eternal commonplaces. It is pretty certain that the same friend would have made the same comment, and probably with less tolerance, had he been a contemporary of that great chatterbox Socrates, who was Lowes Dickinson's ideal man.

What might be called the central chapter of the biography is named " The Socratic Method "; it covers the years 1893-1914, and deals with lecturing, writing, teaching, and social relation- ships. In this last, Mr. Forster's constructive novelist's gift is brilliantly at work, and achieves a great portrait, building the untidy, inartistic, unaccommodating, inconsistent truthfulness of life into a figure not tidied up, not rounded off, but still emerging as a realizable whole, whether he is shown as a shy, silent host giving lunch to a shy undergraduate (Mr. Forster in 1898),

> " We had Winchester cutlets, a sort of elongated rissole to which he was then addicted, but I can remember nothing about the conversation, and probably there was none . . . we sat alone in the large front room silently eating the cutlets and drinking the reddish-brown sauce in which they lay "—

as president of a college discussion society, as educationist, or as eager inquirer into the world's various expressions of the religious instinct. There is a good analysis of his point of view on the relation between intellect and religious intuition.

> " He had the religious temperament, but he hated all the religious weapons. . . . ' God ' and ' Jesus ' and ' Krishna ' trail so many associations and are coloured by so many earthly passions that it is difficult not to be carried away by them and he was more reluctant than his women friends to be carried away. He saw at the end of those famous short words, which boom like a gong out of darkest night— he saw not light, but more darkness, mass-psychology, crowd-cruelty. To be carried

away ? Yes, but in which direction ? Away from the truth or
towards it ? We cannot know, because the tests of knowledge
do not apply. Towards kindness or towards unkindness ?
That we can know, and the sinister record of religious idealism
in the past made him scrutinise his intuitions carefully, and
stick to the intellect, which anyhow sheds less blood.

" One may almost say of him that he held nineteenth-century
opinions in a twentieth-century way. For him, as for the
Victorians, life was a pilgrimage, not an adventure, but he
journeyed without donning their palmer's weeds. It is significant that though he felt the questions of personal immor-
tality and the existence of God to be so important he never got
fussed over them."

He was, in fact, a Victorian agnostic, and joined
the Psychical Research Society, and, as others
have, found that it led him into a " dustbin of the
spirit," a quagmire of toshery (but why didn't he
know that it must ?) in which he faithfully and
painfully grubbed for fragments of truth.

The second half of the book is concerned with
extra-University adventures—travel in America,
in India, and in China; the war, the shock and
disillusionment of which " broke something in
him which was never mended."

" If you feel," he wrote to a friend, " that there is a cause
for it other than mere folly and crime, you are more fortunate
than I am. . . . But if one's whole life had been given up to
trying to establish reason and suddenly the gulf opens and one
finds that the world's ruled by force and wishes to be so, one
feels forlorn indeed and more than forlorn. . . . These things lie
too deep for argument. One is one kind of man or the other."

Not only the war folly of militarists, but the

war idealism of most of his friends, isolated him.
" He was condemned to follow the intellect in a
world which had become emotional." The Christian churches lived up to his gloomiest view of
them. They would not, he wrote bitterly,

> " ever recover any influence, nor do they deserve to. The
> greatest crisis in history has found them without counsel or
> policy or guidance, merely re-echoing the passions of the
> worst crowd. Civilization is perishing, and they look on
> passive and helpless. . . . If there is to be a religion in the
> future it will grow up outside the churches and persecuted by
> them—as indeed is now the case at home. I write all this
> hastily and crudely, and perhaps unwisely."

Rather hasty and crude it was, for it apparently
(but unintentionally, for he excepts them elsewhere)
includes the Quakers among the reprehensible
churches, and is unjustly sweeping about the
others, which are, after all, made up of laity of all
views, including (even then) the most extreme
anti-war. When he writes to a friend working in
France with the Y.M.C.A., " You will find that
the fact of being officially connected with any
religious organization cuts you off from all the
decent English," he seems less a scholar in pursuit of accuracy and precise statement, than a
dreamer seeing facts as he would have them be.
But it was a hot moment, and he did not escape—
perhaps no one did—its fierce exaggerations.

> " He felt, like many actual Christians, that Christ had been
> betrayed by the spirit of nationalism, and when he saw religion
> becoming frankly tribal, and the army chaplain taking no

nonsense from the saint, he believed that it would never recover
its spiritual kingdom."

Worse, from his point of view (for after all he
had always disapproved of " the churches "), was
the *trahison des clercs*, the tide of nationalism and
militarism that swept over the universities. He

" learned once for all that students, those whose business it
would seem to be to keep the light of truth burning in a storm,
are like other men, blindly patriotic, savagely vigilant, cow-
ardly or false when public opinion once begins to run strong."

" He had shirked," Mr. Forster explains, " the
horrors of crowd-psychology, and Cambridge was
now compelling him to view them in surroundings
where he thought they could not occur." His
reaction and chief consolation was to draft, early
in the war, the germ of a scheme for a League of
Nations, which, as Lord Dickinson wrote after
his death, " owes its birth very largely to his
idealism."

Of all this, and his war and post-war writings,
political activities, and personal life, Mr. Forster
makes a very moving and living story, full of the
fine restrained passion and restless, questing
intellectual energy and political consciousness
which were his to the end. He is not set before
us as a perfect character; he is often seen impatient, irritable, embittered, sensitive beyond any
peace of mind. " He was not complacent, and it
would be an error to round off his career com-
placently."

The memoir ends with a half-puzzled epilogue:
what do Goldsworthy Lowes Dickinson's life and
work amount to in importance? A writer of
distinction, but not really great; a publicist and
a worker for civilization, but the League of
Nations, the great object of his work, has, so far,
not succeeded, and "if it fails, he will join
Shelley and the other ghosts who have protested
vainly against the course of doom and fate." As a
philosophic thinker, he has no claim to the front
rank. Not a great heir of fame, he is yet more than
a dear son of memory, for he lives by his vivid
personality and his rare qualities.

It is in the face of odds that his memoir has
come, as it has, off; for the biographer's easy
tools of irony, cool detachment, and mockery,
have not been at hand, could not be employed
together with affection and admiration so deep.
The subject emerges triumphantly without their
help, in objective, detailed, rich and angular life.
The memoir is a labour of love, and would have
bored an egotistic writer to write, for it is entirely
about its subject, and the subject is handled
tenderly, though without piety, and with such
proportion that both dream and business, keeping
nice balance, lucidly emerge. It seems to have
nearly every quality that close knowledge and
understanding can confer, besides those felicities
of style, humour, and imagination whose lack
makes most biographies pedestrian.

It has been sometimes criticized for its omissions, for not giving enough emphasis to the strong and sometimes unhappy emotion that coloured many of its subject's friendships. The answer to this seems to be that the detailed record of strong emotions is too overwhelming, it throws the proportion out of gear; in real life the personality lives through them, is dented and moulded by them, and goes on its way; but in a written record they seem to swamp, to flow over and submerge the fine edges of the intellectual and philosophic outfit which is the essential mind, and falsely suggest, as many novels suggest, a continuous state of soppiness. In other words, it is easier to overstate than to understate emotional life. Mr. Forster has not understated, but he has been reticent, and his reticences do not mislead. And actually the intellectual adventures, and the moments of mystical experience, described here, are far more important to the whole personality than those outgoings of emotion which are common to us all. More of the sonnets, however, might have been quoted; they are not first class, but do convey, in their fusion of intellect and emotion, a side of the writer not so fully shown elsewhere.

The only other writing of Mr. Forster's which much resembles this book is the short obituary note on Roger Fry,* his friend and Lowes Dickinson's; an exquisite piece of portraiture.

* *Abinger Harvest.*

# CHAPTER XVII

## SOME CONCLUSIONS

AS was said at the beginning of this study, in assessing a writer one tries to set him against a background, and to discriminate between what is essentially himself and what are reactions to the impacts made on him by the tendencies and chances of his age. This dual and interlinked ideology—the study, that is, of a man's ideas, and of the ideas surrounding him, and of the way in which they are connected—is worth attempting, however slightly and unsuccessfully. One gets down to the constant problem of the relation between the permanent and the transient, between temperament and circumstance. A man has in his blood certain views, tendencies and impulses, and these will somehow out; the mode of their expression is dictated by the impact of circumstance. In any mind worth considering, there are a set of more or less consistent reactions to the universe, that affect all his ideas. He will hold certain doxies (an old-fashioned word that is neater than the prevalent " ideology," which seems unnecessarily to confuse the doxies with the study of them), and these, their roots ineradicably in the soil of temperament, have their growth, their shape, and the particular flowers which they at various seasons put forth, guided by such erratic gardeners as public and private tendencies and events, the watering-cans and prunings and loppings and distortions of what is called the Age. The native hard common sense and comic sense and anti-sentimentality of Aristophanes emerged by the chance of contemporaneousness as derisive antagonism to the Euripidean ethos and manner; various roots in the complex soul of Dante grew up into such flourishing plants as his hatred of the Florentine government, of local Italian dialects, of all his political and personal enemies, of certain sins and sinners, and as faith in pure and spiritual love, in an avenging God, in a strong united monarchy and papacy, and in the Illustrious Vulgar Tongue. Spenser, who had as roots belief in romance, noble conduct, and beauty, found that these burgeoned, oddly, into the apotheosis of Queen Elizabeth and of the Protestant religion; Richard Crashaw, with the root of passionate piety, grew the flowers of Roman Catholicism, devotion, and glorification of the saints; John Wesley, similarly rooted but differently environed and impacted, grew a plant of devotion of a different species. Sir John Suckling, who naturally believed mainly in Cupid and in winning money at bowls and picquet, was Royalist by force of circumstance, as Milton, whose essential faiths were in liberty, individualism, Latin, music, the higher education of men and the subjection of women, expressed these in passionate pleas for the destruction of prelacy and royalty, for easier divorce, and for the Good Old Cause; to-day he would probably have stood for Parliament as an Independent member and been the secretary of the Council for Civil Liberties. Shelley would have gone to Spain to be brotherly with the Anarchists and tease the Communists, or to Italy, Germany or Russia, to languish in prison for forming revolutionary societies, or to Canada to parade naked with the Doukhobars; Dr. Johnson, who hated Whigs, atheists, Scotchmen, and Americans, would to-day—but one cannot pursue this matter further. All these writers' natural tastes, faiths, humours and prejudices— (or, if you prefer it, postjudices, for it is usual, I suppose, to take a preliminary look at the persons or opinions judged, and, if Swift had not seen his fellow creatures first, he would not have disliked them so much)—flower into doxies apposite to the moment, but what colours their writings is the flower's deep root. From certain root beliefs in Morgan Forster, his political and public views and sympathies naturally grow. He believes, for example, in the permanent value and importance of human beings, and perhaps of their relationships with one another; he believes in culture, that can understand and receive beauty; and he believes in freedom, intellectual, social, and personal.

Human personality and relationships must, of course, be a main concern with all novelists, unlike all poets; for Mr. Forster, they seem at the centre of the business of life. A man not interested in, or attached to, human beings, is to him of petty stature, outside the stream of life. Marco Polo, for instance, unlike Herodotus, was " only a little traveller," for he was " interested in novelties, to the exclusion of human beings . . . he could manage men and conciliate them and outwit them, but they never fascinated him."* Of Swift, " I never liked him much," he writes to Madan Blanchard, the self-marooned mariner. " He didn't care for horses, but he hated people, and used horses for saying so." Speaking of Lytton Strachey, he insists on his belief in affection. " Look back at the *Queen Victoria*, the *Elizabeth and Essex*, the *Portraits in Miniature*. Forget the brilliancy of the pictures, and ask instead what Strachey found valuable in the lives portrayed. Not fame or luxury or fun, though he appreciated all three. Affection, durability. He knew that affection can be ludicrous to the onlooker, and may be tragic in the end, but he never wavered as to its importance, and that such a man should ever have been labelled a cynic really fills one with despair." The durability of friendship: the words

* *Abinger Harvest.*

recall Goldsworthy Lowes Dickinson, whose life was compact of friendships, and who " when he looked back could say with truth that his personal relationships had been enduring."

As has been said earlier, what is mainly wrong with the bad characters in the novels is that they don't like people; they can't fellow. Cecil Vyse " plays tricks on people, on the most sacred form of life that he can find." He despises and sneers; he is " the sort who can't know anyone intimately "; he cares for books and music, but not for people. Mr. Eager, the bad Florence chaplain, also dislikes people. Harriet, the worst character in *Where Angels Fear to Tread*, hates them all the time. So, we feel sure, though he does not spend much time with us, does Gerald Dawes, the bully of *The Longest Journey*. The Wilcoxes' attitude towards people is one of hard, vulgar, good-humoured, contemptuous suspicion, until they are crossed or tricked, when it becomes hard, vulgar, contemptuous anger. It is much the attitude of the English in *A Passage to India* towards the Indians. The Schlegel attitude (except Tibby's, who is bored by people) is one of eager, friendly inquiry, like a dog's, followed on closer acquaintanceship by sympathetic interest, unless they chance to dislike some character. Social and racial barriers do not bother their imaginations, though they may hamper their progress. Margaret believes that it is " personal intercourse, and that alone, that ever hints as a personality beyond our daily vision."

It is in *Howards End* that the creed of the central importance in life of personal relations finds its most convinced statement: the earlier novels have for axis something else; and in *A Passage to India* the position is not so much abandoned as extended, personal intercourse being submerged, even drowned, in the dark seas of racial hostility. Fielding and Aziz cannot be friends; they must go separate ways; Anglo-India stands on one side, India on the other; personal friendship is a detail, an irrelevant affirmation in a huge negation; nothing can be built on it; it is too early, and too late. Centuries of personal discourtesy and mis-understanding have, it is true, played their part in widening the chasm; but could personal friendli-ness have bridged it? Friendship, as Aziz remarks, must wait. Yet there is kindness, " more kindness, and even after that more kind-ness. I assure you it is the only hope." That is the earlier Aziz, before the assaults of injustice have permanently enraged him. Fielding agrees that the constitutional reforms are " beginning at the wrong end." But later he probably agrees with the later Aziz that it is the only end left. The Mrs. Moores will not solve the Indian problem. Yet man must, if he would not be lost, realize his affinity with his fellows. Mr. Forster seems to agree for a while with Mrs. Moore, who " felt

s

increasingly (vision or nightmare ?) that, though people are important, the relations between them are not." But, on the whole, he rejects this; he does believe that human life must be built on affection, and on the integrity of personal relationships. Believing this, an artist must express it as best he may. Music, which conveys more to Mr. Forster than any other art, cannot express people and their relationships; it gives overtones and backgrounds, but not the personal detail. Even had he been a musician, he could not have said all he wanted in music. It had to be expressed in words, which trace the pattern of an imagination richly charged with perceptions of more than words can actually say. I do not know where the *charged* effect of his prose is to be paralleled in English fiction, except in some of the prose of Virginia Woolf, and here and there in D. H. Lawrence's. It is something far more than style, and behind style; it suggests such pressure of thought and meaning on language that no word or phrase is empty, and nothing said or done by any of his creatures is idle. He does not " live in " his characters, or induce his readers to do so; they perform something which his sense of them, and of life, requires, and, in so doing, live for themselves.

Human relationships are with him a large theme. What we call (with a rather crude and impudent exclusiveness) Love, or (with a rather callow and ungrammatical ellipsis) Sex, does not

loom with the conventional and tedious predomin-
ance given it by most imaginative writers. He
handles it now casually, now with a gingerly
aloofness, now with a welcome in which its particular incidence appears submerged or sub-
limated by reverence for it as a token coin of
further and more important immensities. With
kisses, those queer primitive symptoms, his
civilized mind is not happy or at home; nor with
betrothals. Cecil Vyse's first embrace of his Lucy
has already been instanced as improbable even
for the medieval celibate and ascetic that his
creator indicates that he was (for that matter,
there was not much that medieval celibates
and ascetics did not know about embracing;
they could have given the Greeks points on this
topic any day). Mr. Forster has more successful
kissing, bigger and better passion, than this, in
the same book, for Lucy is also kissed by George,
who is not a medieval celibate, and this comes off,
both as kissing and as the key that opens the
windows on to the view. Their love is not taken
as an end in itself, it is a spiritual victory. All the
same, it is the only example in Mr. Forster's
writings of triumphant, whole-souled and gratified passion. Elsewhere, passion plays a less
creditable role; either it is divorced from reason
and the spirit, a carnal entanglement and confusion, Lowes Dickinson's " queen of night en-
gendering her dark broods beyond mind," or, as

in the story *The Eternal Moment*, it is a remembered
peak from which those who stood romantically on
it slide rapidly down, to forget it, or recall it later
with tenderness or derision according to their
natures. For Miss Raby in this story it had been,
she later saw, the greatest moment in her life, that
declaration of passion from a young Italian mountain porter now grown a vulgar middle-aged
concierge. It had led to nothing, except, romanticized in her memory, to her own development;
therefore she and Mr. Forster can treat it with
respect. Had she married the young man, it
would have led to tragedy, brief or prolonged and
would have become, in retrospect, ignominious; it
was an eternal moment only because a sterile one.
In *Where Angels Fear to Tread*, where passion is
not frustrated, it leads to fatal enchainment for the
vulgar Lilia, who is unhappy for evermore; and
for prim Caroline, who also falls into it, it is a
fruitless catastrophe of the affections. Later, she
will, we feel, remember it with wistful astonish-
ment. Passion, less fortunately insulated from
consequences, traps Rickie Elliot into going the
longest journey with one sad friend, perhaps a
jealous foe. Rickie, reading about this during his
engagement, feels Shelley

" a little inhuman. Half a mile off two lovers were keeping
company where all the villagers could see them. They cared
for no one else ; they felt only the pressure of each other, and
so progressed, silent and oblivious, across the land. He felt

them to be nearer the truth than Shelley. Even if they suffered or quarrelled, they would have been nearer the truth."

Soon after marriage, if not before, he changes his mind, and agrees again with Shelley. True, he is married to an appalling woman. But Mr. Forster's view in this book is, I think, more or less that of Ansell—that civilized men cannot and should not be permanently happy in marriage. Even Stephen, who is not a civilized man, is happy in marriage not because he is married to the one woman, but because he is playing his part in the great procession of the earth, he is a husband and father. " She should never have all my thoughts," he explains to Rickie of the potential wife whom he would like.

" ' Out of no disrespect to her, but because all one's thoughts can't belong to any single person. . . . You can't own people. At least a fellow can't. It may be different for a poet. And I want to marry someone, and don't yet know who she is, which a poet again will tell you is disgusting. . . . It's something rather outside that makes one marry, if you follow me : not exactly oneself. . . .'

" Romantic love is greater than this. There are men and women—we know it from history—who have been born into the world for each other, and for no one else, who have accomplished the longest journey locked in one another's arms. . . . Eternal union, eternal ownership—these are tempting baits for the average man. He swallows them, will not confess his mistake, and—perhaps to cover it—cries ' dirty cynic ' at such a man as Stephen."

Passion in this book plays a traitor part to those

less sensible than Stephen. It flashes before Rickie's dazzled eyes in a moment of embracement between two commonplace barbarians, Gerald and Agnes, and turns his world to glory, music and flame.

> " Music flowed past him like a river. He stood at the springs of creation and heard the primeval monotony. . . . In full unison was Love born, flame of the flame, flushing the dark river beneath him and the virgin snows above. His wings were infinite, his youth eternal; the sun was a jewel on his finger as he passed it in benediction over the world. . . . Was Love a column of fire? Was he a torrent of song? Was greater than either—the touch of a man or woman?
>
> " It was the merest accident that Rickie had not been disgusted. But this he could not know."

Thus a prey to over-excitement, Rickie is snared, making an eternal glory out of an animal impulse, whose remembered illumination lights later his own path into the prison. The flares die down, ashes and bitterness are left.

Poor Rickie is eminently trappable; any piece of romantic idealism serves him for cheese and shoots the bolt behind him. By the time Margaret Schlegel arrives on the scene, civilized, sensible, experimental and aware, trapping is less easy. Margaret may enjoy the cheese, but she knows it for what it is, and will not be caught unawares. She is, in fact, too busy trying to connect the cheese with the bread that should accompany it to let it trap her. She will not have it by itself; passion must be part of tenderness, part of love.

Mr. Wilcox's isolated, disconnected embraces displease her. Without the connection that she wanted him to make between passion and tenderness,

> " we are meaningless fragments, half monks, half beasts, unconnected arches that have never joined into a man. With it love is born, and alights on the highest curve, glowing against the grey, sober against the fire. Happy the man who sees from either aspect the glory of those outspread wings. The roads of his soul lie clear, and he and his friends shall find easy going. . . . Only connect, and the beast and the monk, robbed of the isolation that is life to either, will die."

It will be remarked that love has climbed a good way since his questionable status in *The Longest Journey*; and his rather Wattsian figure here is more sublime and elevated than it appeared even to the impassioned, but simple, Lucy and George, who did not bother about civilizing or connecting the component elements in their love, but merely desired to come together and remain so. Margaret, a highbrow prig (it is part of her charm) believed too in love as the supreme thing in life, but it had to be of the best brand.

> " She knew that out of Nature's device we have built a magic that shall win us immortality. Far more mysterious than the call of sex to sex is the tenderness that we throw into that call; far wider is the gulf between us and the farmyard than between the farmyard and the garbage that nourishes it. . . . ' Man did produce one jewel,' the gods will say, and, saying, will give us immortality."

This view is not endorsed by Mrs. Moore in

*A Passage to India*, and we feel that Mr. Forster has advanced to her view of the affair.

> " She felt . . . that in particular too much fuss has been made over marriage ; centuries of carnal embracement, yet man is no nearer to understanding man."

Adela Quested, concerned less with the general question of the value of love, than with her personal problem, did she love Ronny, ponders it much as Margaret had done, but with less vivacity.

> " There was esteem and animal contact at dusk, but the emotion that links them was absent. Ought she to break her engagement off ? "

But here she and Margaret part company. " She was inclined to think not," not because, as Margaret had thought, she could improve her lover's affection and her own—she lacked Margaret's enthusiasm for and faith in improvement—but because

> " she wasn't convinced that love is necessary to a successful union. If love is everything, few marriages would survive the honeymoon. . . . She felt a bit dashed."

As to Mrs. Moore, she grows, under the combined influence of ill health and the Marabar caves, more and more petulant with the whole silly business.

> " Why all this marriage, marriage ? . . . The human race would have become a single person centuries ago if marriage was any use. And all this rubbish about love, love in a church, love in a cave, as if there is the least difference, and I held up from my business over such trifles ! "

Less crossly, Fielding also dismisses marriage as irrelevant.

" Marriage is too absurd in any case. It begins and continues for such very slight reasons. The social business props it up on one side, and the theological business on the other, but neither of them are marriage, are they ? I've friends who can't remember why they married, no more can their wives. I suspect that it mostly happens haphazard, though afterwards various noble reasons are invented. About marriage I am cynical."

Later, after his own marriage for love, his cynicism fails him. He loves his wife with passion, she him with less; but he knows that passion is not enough, and wants to establish some link between them, " that link outside either partici-pant that is necessary to every relationship." In a few years he will very likely be echoing Mrs. Moore—" The human race would have become a single person centuries ago if marriage was any use. And all this rubbish about love. . . ." The problem of the oneness of the human race is not, in fact, to be so solved, and it is the human race that matters, and matters increasingly, to Mr. Forster, who has steadily moved out from the centre to the circumference, from faith in indivi-dual personal relationships as the axis of a troubled world to tentative speculations on more general human relations. As to love, it is infinitely various in kind, and there is room for every kind. " People," says Margaret, " are far more dif-ferent than is pretended." For some, sexual love is the chief; for others parental love; for others, the love of friends. Others, again, move outside humanity altogether, and love God. Some even love places best. "It is part of the battle against sameness." Sex love, therefore, falls into line, takes a modest place among the others, is not the supreme motive force in any of the novels except *A Room With a View*; though he made it, here, a fine full-blooded surge of the blood and senses, as well as "mattering intellectually," and though he could call it "love felt and returned, love which our bodies exact and our hearts have transfigured, love which is the most real thing that we shall ever meet," it does not really matter intensely to him; and here, I think, he is in line with the tendency of our age.

Also in the extension of his concern with individuals to that concern with large numbers of them together that is called politics. The word, set down, looks foolish, as if Mr. Forster were an election candidate and we were putting to him questions about his views. Yet "politics," after all, have been supposed to be, contrary to all experience of them, "that sublime science which embraces for its object the happiness of mankind" —an embrace as defective as any of those which Mr. Forster records—and any writer who is not a dullard or an impervious egoist must have political opinions, though he need side with no party and subscribe to no political formula or doxy. Mr.

Forster, who definitely respects and likes the human race, believes in liberty for it. He believes in this with passionate conviction; one feels that it matters more to him than anything else. He believes in it both in theory and practice, unlike Dr. Johnson, and many other Tories, who treat liberty with a kind of contemptuous empiricism, as if all that mattered were practical liberty in action, which, say they, can usually be wrested by the individual out of even tyrannical laws. " They make a rout," said Johnson, " about universal liberty, without considering that all that is to be valued, or indeed can be enjoyed by individuals, is *private* liberty. Now, Sir, there is the liberty of the Press, which you know is a constant topic. Suppose you and I and two hundred more were restrained from printing our thoughts, what then ? What proportion would that restraint upon us bear to the private happiness of the nation ? "

A kind of sophistry, as Boswell disapprovingly remarked, in which the Doctor delighted to indulge himself; and the kind of sophistry which usually means that the indulger does not really like the thought of much liberty for most of his fellow creatures. Mr. Forster, who does like the thought, makes a rout about liberty; an increasing rout as liberty suffers increasingly dire assaults in this sinister age. He has written and spoken on English freedom, a little jewel set in a sullen sea, precious but limited, " merely a habit of life, confined to people living in England or under English conditions . . . nor do we allow it to be adopted by such races as we control." And even in England it is maimed by the inability of the hungry and the homeless to enjoy it. Still, it is a fine affair, and we guard it jealously from the fierce assaults now being made on it, from, he says, three enemies—Fascism and Communism, which both " believe in dictators and drill and monkeying about with mass-psychology," and a third, less defined but still more dangerous enemy, which he calls " Fabio-Fascism, the Mussolini spirit working quietly away behind the freedom of constitutional forms," undermining a little here, a little there.

> " Our freedom to-day has more to fear from enlightened authoritarians like Lord Hailsham or Lord Lloyd or Lord Trenchard than from Sir Oswald Mosley or Sir Stafford Cripps. . . . Foreign imports will probably cancel each other out. It is the home product which may need sympathetic study."

So Mr. Forster plays his part in such sympathetic (I should not myself have selected the adjective) watching as is performed by the Council for Civil Liberties and other bodies. He protests against the Sedition Bill; against any extension of suppression anywhere, including the suppression of books called obscene.* Such literary suppression

* See his Foreword to *The Banned Books of England,* by Alec Craig (Allen & Unwin, 1937).

is the gravamen of his address to the International Congress of Writers at Paris in 1935.* Some suppressed books are bad, some good; it makes no difference, they should not be suppressed for obscenity unless they are obscene, possibly not even then, and anyhow who is to decide? Like Milton, he would certainly feel, of any censor, " Who shall warrant me his judgment ? " and would want to ding a licensed book a coit's length from him. His detestation of nosiness even occasionally sinks his art, as in the sketch called *Mrs. Grundy at the Parkers*,* one of his very rare examples of falliloquence.

His libertarianism is rooted partly in his value for individuality and the individual; and out of the same root grows his mistrust of generalizations and party cries, " the cries of ignorant armies that clash by night." Regiment, beyond the minimum, is monstrous in his eyes, it crushes all, or nearly all, that is worth having in human life. He is really a liberal, an early twentieth-century liberal, like his own Schlegels, to whom liberalism means freedom. Margaret Schlegel, walking in Hertfordshire, perceived a freedom in its contours, and thought (a fanciful creature), " Left to itself, this county would vote liberal." Even now, when liberalism seems (to all but liberals) a lost battle, living only for a problematical victory in a highly dubious future, Mr. Forster is still a liberal.

* *Abinger Harvest.*

So he informed the Paris Congress, admitting his attitude to be of the past, and that most of his hearers probably felt it " waste of time to talk about freedom and tradition when the economic structure of society is unsatisfactory." He is, he says, " a writer of the individualistic and liberalizing type," which will be swept away by another war, and after another war, " if there is an after, the task of civilization will be carried on by people whose training has been different from my own." He is a liberal, hating and scorning Fascism as wholly evil, dreading and disliking Communism as a possibly necessary future. Three paths, he says (in June, 1934) lie before us at the present moment. There is

> " the present order, which I prefer, because I have been brought up in it. I like Parliament and democracy. I should like England and Europe to muddle on as they are, without the international explosion that would end them. . . . In the second place, there is Communism, an alternative which will destroy all I care for and could only be reached through violence, yet it might mean a new order where younger people could be happy and the head and the heart have a chance to grow. There, and on no other horizon, the boys and girls might return to the cliff and dance. If my own world smashes, Communism is what I would like in its place, but I shall not bless it until I die. And, thirdly, there is Fascism, leading only into the blackness which it has chosen as its symbol, into smartness and yapping out of orders, and self-righteous brutality, into social as well as international war. It means change without hope. . . . Our immediate duty is to stop it."

To this duty, grown so immediate and so urgent,

Mr. Forster has of late years, like other writers, been drawn. The defence of democracy, liberty and culture against Fascism: it has become a slogan. One resents it, this horrid ism, this dark and dreadful doxy, that has flung its brutal shadow over the world, distorting our view of culture, turning it into a kind of political vendetta or preventive campaign against an enemy that would crush it. Culture should be a thing pursued and furthered, not " defended "; it should not be bound up in our minds with any political party or colour, the fine flowers in its garden should bloom regardless of what political constitution obtains, and those who can cultivate any corner of that garden should, we may think, do so with a single mind; perhaps they would be well advised just now not even to read the newspapers. Yes, comes the answer, and while the gardeners are thus employed the garden is broken into and trampled and fouled by the wild boars. . . . It is infinitely complicated, and Mr. Forster, like many others who care for culture, has heard this warning and responds to it by active self-identification with anti-boar defensive activities. His garden must necessarily suffer a little from neglect while he is thus engaged, lose some of its finer blooms, which there is not time or concentration to cultivate. But there it is, something must go, he would say, and better some of these fine blooms than the whole garden. The trouble is, as he admits, that the better alternative, Communism, would also annihilate many of the blooms. The totalitarian state, the herd oneness, the concentration on political unity and social and cultural toeing of the line, the rule of the callow propagandist mind, these " will destroy all I care for," but it may be worth while. Fascism " does evil that evil may come "; Communism does evil that good may come, and the evil may have to be endured. There may, in the end, after all the bitterness and violence, be culture of a kind for all, even if freedom perishes.

On this question of the merits of Communism, Mr. Forster sees between him and many of his friends the gulf of years. In middle life, one is all for liberty, one dislikes dictatorships of any kind, even well-intentioned ones.

" I am not a Communist, though perhaps I might be if I was a younger and a braver man, for in Communism I can see hope. It does many things that I think evil, but I know that it intends good. I am actually what my age and my upbringing have made me—a bourgeois who adheres to the British constitution, adheres to it rather than supports it, and the fact that this isn't dignified doesn't worry me. I do care about the past, and I do care about the preservation and the extension of freedom."

So the individual must, in this difficult hour,

" even if his body be bound refuse to merge his soul in totalitarian emotions. Thus alone will he keep ready for a better day, when the body as well as the soul may be free."

It is the attitude of many liberals: to avert

worse, and should it seem necessary, he will be a communist *malgré lui*, but it all seems a great pity, and if only our democracy could and would make a society fit for human beings to live in, how much better it would be! He knows that it probably cannot do so; traditions of selfish clinging to possessions and blind conservatism are too strong for us. We each cling to our bit of property, those of us who have any, and for the effect of property on its owner, read that gay jest, *My Wood*.* Property produces men of weight; it makes its owners feel that it should be larger; and that they must fence it from intruders.

> " I shall wall in and fence out until I really taste the sweets of property. Enormously stout, endlessly avaricious, pseudo-creative, intensely selfish, I shall weave upon my forehead the quadruple crown of possession, until those nasty Bolshies come and take it off again and thrust me aside into the outer darkness."

No, it will not do. To put it briefly, he minds too much about the poor to cling whole-heartedly to our ramshackle democracy.

> " You," he addresses them, " are the slush and dirt on which our civilization rests, which it treads underfoot daily. . . .
>
> " The misery goes on, the feeble impulses of good return to the sender, and far away, in some other category, far away from the snobbery and glitter in which our souls and bodies have been entangled, is forged the instrument of the new dawn."

A grim dawn enough; but it may make life

* *Abinger Harvest.*

T

tolerable in some distant, costly future, for the Leonard Basts, all the poor, of whom he wrote in *Howards End* that it did not do to think.

Then there is war; another unthinkable of which we must now constantly think. The thought of it haunts Mr. Forster, as it must haunt all rational and sensitive people, as an obscene nightmare. Writing of it two years ago, he weighed one against another several lines of policy. There is the line of heavy armaments.

> "An adequate defence force is the treasure lying at the foot of the devil's rainbow: it moves away and away until civilization follows it over the precipice. But this will not hinder the government. We shall before long be in a position to burn and poison many more foreigners than we can at present, and to destroy foreign towns and works of art more promptly and thoroughly. No one wishes to do this, but it is all that rearmament can do. Mutual fear will increase, and sooner or later we, or the enemy of the moment, will get the jumps and take the initiative. It is a toss-up whether we ruin his capital before he ruins London, but both of us have a good chance of succeeding almost simultaneously, and neither of us has much chance of making peace afterwards."

The second line is to have only a small, inadequate armed force. This seems to him " slightly less imbecile and suicidal than the first." For it will mean that we shall not take the initiative, and the enemy

> " though tempted to take it, may reflect, since defence no longer exists, that we shall be able to burn and poison a few of his people while he is burning and poisoning a large number of ours. . . . It may be that governments will . . . stay their

hands, and remain in the condition known as ' sullen hate.'
Sullen hate is not too bad as things go ; private lives can be led
tolerably under its cloud. It is when the cloud blazes and the
thunderbolts fall that all decency perishes."

It might, he adds, be safer to have no armed force
at all, but there is no chance of this, whereas a
small one is achievable. As to the National
Government, " unless some change of heart comes
over them, we are bound to be involved in a major
war before their tenure expires."

There is a third line—Communism. He is
" impressed by the Communist argument which
ascribes war to the capitalist system," and though
" it is possible to argue that even if Communism
could be established wars would continue," he
does not regard this as an answer. He is a little
troubled and inconclusive here, and happier
with the psychological policy urged by Gerald
Heard—preventing war not from without but
from within, though he cannot take this either as
an immediate talisman. He is, in fact, in the position of thousands of other bewildered and frightened people, who see little hope of staying the
monster's advance. What can one do, he asks,
beyond not investing money in manufactures that
may be used for armaments, and protesting against
that " annual imbecility," the Aldershot Tattoo
and the Olympia Tournament ?

" I can say nothing new against war, and I can do scarcely
anything to prevent it. . . . All other evils will right, or may

right, themselves. Social injustice and poverty can be cured, the evils in personal life can be righted by death. But for war, under modern conditions, there seems no death ; once generated, it must galvanize a whole continent into madness and pain. This is obvious, and whether we are agreed that war is inevitable or not, we are all agreed as to its character. And yet I am asked to buy tickets for an ' entertainment ' where some athletes in fancy dress will play games with that curious survival the horse, and so work me up into a state of mind which bears no relation to the fact. I am to be made to feel that war is glorious and ennobling. . . .

" Any Government which really worked for peace would have forbidden all tournaments and tattoos. Their psychological effect on simple people is appalling. . . . Let them show the effect of vesicant dew on a girls' school—upon two girls' schools, our own and the enemy's. The fathers and mothers in the audience might begin to understand at last."

Since he wrote this, air-raid instructions have ensured that there should be few illusions in people's minds as to what to expect in war. But his final counsel, or prophecy, of despair would still hold: if war comes, " many individuals would claim and exercise the right to put those they love out of pain and to commit suicide." Meanwhile, and till it comes, " the universe being very complicated and large, we had better spend a bit of our time rather than all of it in peace work, and spend the balance in doing other things and in enjoying ourselves."

If war is the deadliest evil, imperialism, materialism, and size-worship are the vulgarest. When Germany beat France, and turned into an

Empire, a commercial power with a forward policy and colonies, Ernst Schlegel* left her and naturalized himself in England. " It was his hope that the clouds of materialism obscuring the Fatherland would part in time, and the mild intellectual light re-emerge."

" Your Pan-Germanism " (he says to a German nephew), " is no more imaginative than is our Imperialism over here. It is the vice of a vulgar mind to be thrilled by bigness, to think that a thousand square miles are a thousand times more wonderful than one square mile. . . . That is not imagination. No, it kills it. When their poets over here try to celebrate bigness they are dead at once, and naturally. Your poets too are dying, your philosophers, your musicians, to whom Europe has listened for two hundred years. Gone. Gone with the little courts that nurtured them—gone with Esterhaz and Weimar."

Size, empire, vastness, conquest, all the Kipling idols—how he dislikes them! Napoleon, Cecil Rhodes, Crœsus, Cæsars of all kinds, for these he has a half-amused, half-appalled irony. As Stephen Wonham protests, " I can't gallop a horse out of this view without tiring it, so what is the point of a boundless continent ? " Mr. Pembroke of Sawston, being not a nice character, lectures the school on the size and splendour of the Empire; and when he paused, there were sobs from a little boy " who was regretting a villa in Guildford and his mother's half-acre of garden." Patriotism, yes, for one loves the fields

* *Howards End*

and woods of one's home; this happy breed of men, this little world; imperialism is the negation of all that, and nationalism is the devil. It is nationalism that he means when he says, " between patriotism and poetry there is a profound, if unfortunate, antipathy. The poems that have helped men to be brave and honest and fierce are seldom beautiful. ' God Save the King ' is not beautiful. ' We Want Eight and We Won't Wait ' is little better. Yet both of them have made history." He is, it is apparent, a Little Englander; also a Little German, a Little Italian, a Little Francer; he would like all countries dwindled to a homely size, not only because they would be safer so, but because they would have a finer civilization, more beauty.

Beauty, civilization, culture: these matter more than anything else; liberty matters because it guards these, as well as guarding the rights of the ordinary human being to do what he wishes. It is æsthetic pleasures that count most intensely. Music first; then literature, art, beauty of colour and shape. As fully as Pater's, and without Pater's conscious and mannered decorativeness, his books are charged with æsthetic emphasis. Because it includes the whole of life, it is never " arty "; he is every time with the simple philistine against the pretentious cultured; and because it is witty it is never either empurpled or remote. Beauty is not an aim but a satisfaction: it props, as Matthew

Arnold said, " in these bad days my mind." In the
bad days of the war, it was possible to be consoled
and relieved by reading Huysmans.

> " Oh, the relief of a world which lived for its sensations and
> ignored the will—the world of des Esseintes ! Was it deca-
> dent ? Yes, and thank God. Yes ; here again was a human
> being who had time to feel and experience with his feelings, to
> taste and smell and arrange books and fabricate flowers, and be
> selfish and himself. The waves of edifying bilge rolled off me,
> the newspapers ebbed ; Professor Cramb, that profound
> philosopher, and Raemaekers, that inspired artist, floated out
> into an oblivion which, thank God, has since become per-
> manent, and something resembling reality took their place.
> Perhaps it was not real, but it was not helpful, and in 1917
> that was enough to make me repeat . . . ' Thank God.' "*

He thanked God also for the early poems of
Mr. T. S. Eliot; for " what, in that world of
gigantic horror, was tolerable except the slighter
gestures of dissent?"* The later T. S. Eliot "has
gone both beyond me and behind"; his art,
delicate and remote, has increasingly declared
itself rooted in a culture and in values not too
sympathetic to liberal agnostics. The early poems, as
delicate and remote, affirmed less, protested more.

Culture. It is a smug, silly, pompous word, a
little *mal entouré*. Like General Göring, when I
hear it I feel like reaching for a revolver. " A for-
bidding word," Mr. Forster finds it, " which
suggests anthropology or the University Extension movement. I have to use it," he adds,

* *Abinger Harvest*

" knowing of none better, to describe the various beautiful and interesting objects which men have made in the past, and handed down to us, and which some of us are hoping to hand on. Many people despise them."

He is, I think, wrong here; scarcely anyone despises culture, but some people cannot understand it and do not try; also, everyone means by it a different thing; not all culture would include the reading of Dante, which he makes a test case.

> " If people are giving him up (and I think they are), it is a sign that they are throwing culture overboard, owing to the roughness of the water, and will reach the further bank sans Dante, sans Shakespeare and sans everything."

This sounds like, and is, a cry from the past, from another and more distant bank, from across another and rougher gulf; it is the voice of pre- not post-war culture. " Sans everything " is far too much. It is possible to throw over Dante, and even Shakespeare, and indeed any other writer, and yet have a culture rich, intelligent and advanced, and to dislike as much as anyone can rubbishy literature, music and art. Those whose minds are not propped by Dante, Milton, Matthew Arnold, and Beethoven, can sometimes find support in Epstein, Donne (this magnificent divine has in the last thirty years been restored to the fashionable pulpit where three centuries ago he was the rage), Stravinsky, and Colonel de Basil's ballet: all cultural objects which Mr. Forster, too, no doubt, admires, for the older culture has the advantage that it accepts the newer more often than the new the older. Such acceptance narrows the gulf across which writers of one decade talk to writers of another; for Mr. Forster it is not a wide gulf, but it is there, a little bank-dividing brook; his voice, for all its personal individuality, is rather different from what it would have been had he been born thirty, or even twenty, years later, though less different from what it would have been twenty or thirty years earlier. It has a kind of suavity— a poor word, but it implies something, some note of courteous, if demurring, civility, that, whatever it is, is not the tone of these blunt, uncompromising, undecorated days. His very accuracy and truthfulness is a truthfulness arrived at by light and delicate probing; his wit has more of the tea-cup, less of the tankard.

Both his faiths and his denials are rooted in an older culture. His religious scepticism is of the old liberal, anti-clerical, Cambridge type; it has deep roots, and puts out luxuriant shoots. To organized religions he is gaily or sadly unfair. " It is impossible to be fair-minded when one has faith—religious creeds have shown this," he says. And difficult, of course, even when one hasn't. Mystical religion he understands; it has roots in the imagination; Hindu worship, Christian worship. Moslem worship, they all flower from men's spirit of love or of poetry. Creeds and doctrines cramp and warp this spirit, warring against the free growth of the mind; observing their work down the ages, he fears and dislikes them; unable to forgive their intolerance, stupidities, cruelties, squabbling, and spilt blood, he is less than just to the aspirations, poetry and love which have made some men condone and understate their darker side: it is a nice balance, which few have been able precisely to observe. Because the Christian church has had power in Europe for so long, and has misused so much of it, he is more impatient of it than of other theocracies—the Greek, Hindu or Moslem, for instance. Many of the less estimable characters of whom he writes, such as Athanasius, the patriarch Basil and his desert monks who murdered Hypatia, Timothy the Cat, and the Reverend Cuthbert Eager, are already in Holy Orders; others, such as Mr. Pembroke of Sawston school, enter them. Definitely, he does not like clergymen; even Mr. Beebe, a nice one, turns queer at the last, his cloth being too much for him; and, when the boys and girls can " dance on the cliffs," it means that there is no priest on the island. His humanist, liberal, classical mind welcomes religion as spirit but not as doctrine, not as creed; perhaps it welcomes no creeds of any kind, only the spirit behind them. In an age when men are sharply divided by definite creeds, political, economic, religious, when many of our best minds are communist, others Christian,

others this or that, he stands outside all the orches-
tras, all the excited, gesticulatory conductors,
playing on his own instrument his own airs.

How much have his instrument and his airs
influenced other players ? Most players sensitive
to sound must have had their own performance,
or their attempted performance, a little affected
by his melodies, by the new meanings he has given
to phrase and counterpoint and air. He has, to
drop analogy, put English prose on a plane in
many ways new. But he has founded no school;
his style has not, like Henry James's, or
Meredith's, or Lytton Strachey's or Tchekov's,
or Ernest Hemingway's, spawned; it is not
mannered enough for that, and the mind behind
it is too rare to be successfully aped. His influence is rather permeative, like a dye, than an
outside model that can be copied.

What he will write next cannot be guessed.
If it should be another novel of the contemporary
scene, it would be exciting, for the contemporary
scene has changed its features so remarkably since
1910, when he wrote his last novel of English
contemporary life. He might catch its flickering
aspect before the next great cataclysm, as it spins
rather dizzily between light and shade, appre-
hensively yet not without the doomed man's pride
in coming doom, frightened yet a little complacent, with our " look what's going to happen
to us, was there ever such a time, no never,"

idealistic yet cynical in our grim acceptances, still shocked, yet more and more stunned into the callous torpor with which barbarians survey the horrid world that they have made, sullen Frank-ensteins gaping at the crazy homicidal figure of their monster.

I do not know if there is anyone else now writing who has just the right mirror to catch all these shifting reflections, public events and passions impacting on private, private distorted by public. Neither does one know if he has; the affair may have got already too queer and restive and out of hand. It needs an artist who neither lets himself be rattled by the imposing noises off, nor is deaf to their meaning to the individual life. Never has such stabilizing imagination as his been more needed to focus and interpret the human scene. Presently it may be too late for this particular interpreter; neither that murderous chaos to which we so confidently look, nor that as yet dubious re-arrangement of society which he has called (vision or nightmare ? he does not know, but thinks both) " the new dawn," will throw down suitable reflections for his mirror, they would both crack it. The future will be someone else's pigeon. The present might still be his, if he would attempt it.

# BIBLIOGRAPHY

*Novels.*

Where Angels Fear to Tread (Blackwood) 1905
The Longest Journey (Blackwood) 1907
A Room with a View (Arnold) 1908
Howards End (Arnold) 1910
A Passage to India (Arnold) 1924

*Short Stories.*

The Celestial Omnibus (Sidgwick & Jackson) 1911
(contains The Story of a Panic, The Other Side of the Hedge,
The Celestial Omnibus, Other Kingdom, The Curate's Friend,
The Road from Colonnus)
The Story of the Siren (Hogarth Press) 1920
The Eternal Moment (Sidgwick & Jackson) 1928
(contains The Machine Stops, The Point of It, Mr. Andrews,
Co-ordination, The Story of the Siren, The Eternal Moment)
Collected Short Stories of E. M. Forster (Sidgwick & Jackson) 1948

*History.*

Alexandria: A History and a Guide (Whitehead Morris, Alexandria)
1922
Pharos and Pharillon (Hogarth Press) 1923
Notes on Egypt, in the pamphlet, The Government of Egypt (Labour
Research Department) 1920

*Biography.*

Goldsworthy Lowes Dickinson (Arnold) 1934
A Letter to Madan Blanchard (pamphlet) (Hogarth Press) 1931
Desmond MacCarthy (pamphlet) (Mill House Press) 1952
Marianne Thornton (Arnold) 1956

*General.*

Anonymity : An Enquiry (Hogarth Press) 1925
Aspects of the Novel (Arnold) 1927
Abinger Harvest (Arnold) 1936
Two Cheers for Democracy (Arnold) 1951
The Hill of Devi (Arnold) 1953
Tourism v. Thuggism (pamphlet) (Waterlow) 1957


*Libretto.*

Billy Budd. Opera in Four Acts. Music by Benjamin Britten. Libretto
    by E. M. Foster and Eric Crozier. Adapted from the story by
    Herman Melville (Boosey & Hawkes) 1951


*Introductions, etc.*

For details of E. M. Forster's numerous Introductions, Prefaces and
    Contributions to works by other writers, see B. J. Kirkpatrick,
    *A Bibliography of E. M. Forster* (Hart-Davis) 1968

# INDEX